Tales That Teach

Other Books by
Kirsten A. Roggenkamp and Heather Blaire

Boldly Brave: God's Courageous Champions

The Radical Rescue

Securely Strong: God's Faithful Friends

Tales That Teach

by **Kirsten A. Roggenkamp and Heather Blaire**

Pacific Press®
Publishing Association

Nampa, Idaho | www.pacificpress.com

Cover design: ChristianMediaOutlet

Cover design resources: © Niks Ads, Jacek Chabraszewski, kmiragaya, khwanchai, michaeljung, AntonioDiaz / Adobe Stock

Interior design: Aaron Troia

Illustration credits:

GoodSalt.com: 12, 14, 15, 31, 44, 50, 51, 54, 59, 72, 76, 80, 98, 101, 106, 108, 125

GettyImages.com: 11, 17, 19, 20, 22, 23, 24, 26, 27, 29, 32, 35, 36, 37, 39, 40, 41, 43, 46, 47, 49, 55, 57, 58, 62, 63, 66, 67, 69, 71, 73, 75, 79, 81, 83, 84, 85, 88, 89, 91, 92, 95, 96, 99, 102, 105, 109, 111, 113, 114, 116, 117, 120, 121, 124, 127, 128, 12, 14, 15, 31, 44, 50, 51, 54, 59, 72, 76, 80, 98, 101, 106, 108, 125

The authors assume full responsibility for the accuracy of all facts and quotations as cited in this book.

To order additional copies of this book, call toll-free 1-800-765-6955, or visit AdventistBookCenter.com.

Library of Congress Cataloging-in-Publication Data

Names: RoggenKamp, Kirsten, author. | Blaire, Heather, author.
Title: Tales that teach / Kirsten A. Roggenkamp and Heather Blaire.
Description: Nampa, Idaho : Pacific Press Publishing Association, [2023] |
Audience: Grades 4-6 | Summary: "The parables of Jesus, retold for children" — Provided by publisher.
Identifiers: LCCN 2023030611 | ISBN 9780816369553 (paperback) | ISBN 9780816369560 (ebook)
Subjects: LCSH: Bible—Parables—Juvenile literature. | Bible—Study and teaching—Juvenile literature. | Parables—Juvenile literature. | Bible stories—New Testament—Juvenile literature. | Jesus Christ—Parables—Juvenile literature.
Classification: LCC BS680.P3 R64 2023 | DDC 226.8—dc23/eng/20230801
LC record available at https://lccn.loc.gov/2023030611

August 2023

Dedication

To our grandchildren.

May you find and claim the
freedom Jesus offers.

So if the Son sets you free, you will be free indeed.
—John 8:36

Contents

Acknowledgments

We are grateful for Ellen White's books *Christ's Object Lessons* and *The Desire of Ages*. They helped to guide our understanding of the spiritual lessons in the parables of Jesus.

We are indebted to Kenneth E. Bailey—who was the emeritus research professor of Middle Eastern New Testament studies at the Tantur Ecumenical Institute in Jerusalem, who lived in the Middle East for forty years—for his detailed research and insight into the parables of Jesus, as shared in his books *Jesus Through Middle Eastern Eyes: Cultural Studies in the Gospels* (InterVarsity Press, 2008) and *The Cross and the Prodigal: Luke 15 Through the Eyes of Middle Eastern Peasants* (InterVarsity Press, 2005). His books provided us with valuable information as we wrote the stories in this book.

Many thanks to Lisa Butler and Debra Stottlemyer for their support and encouragement.

We deeply appreciate the talented editors and designers at Pacific Press for transforming our manuscript into this book.

Introduction

One day some parents brought their little children to Jesus so he could touch and bless them. But when the disciples saw this, they scolded the parents for bothering him.

Then Jesus called for the children and said to the disciples, "Let the children come to me. Don't stop them! For the Kingdom of God belongs to those who are like these children. I tell you the truth, anyone who doesn't receive the Kingdom of God like a child will never enter it."

—Luke 18:15–17, NLT

What a beautiful scene it must have been to see Jesus blessing the children. Hopeful parents asked the new Rabbi to validate the importance of their sons and daughters. Jesus expressed the value of these children in two ways. First, He spent time with them. The disciples thought Jesus was too busy for such an insignificant task, but they didn't understand. To Jesus, children are a treasure, and taking time to bless them was—and still is—a moment of delight. Second, during their time together, Jesus shared a parable about His kingdom, prompting His listeners to learn from little ones: "For the Kingdom of God belongs to those who are like these children" (Luke 18:16, NLT). In blessing the children, Jesus also blessed the parents who asked for His time.

In His sermon on the mount, Jesus ended with a

story about two builders. Jesus explained, "Therefore everyone who hears these words of mine and puts them into practice is like a wise man who built his house on the rock" (Matthew 7:24). That statement creates the foundation for this book. The lessons of His kingdom found in His stories are very important to learn, remember, and apply. So we wondered whether personalizing the parables by adding names, a character or two, conversations, and imaginative details would make the stories come alive for the children (and parents) of today. We also asked ourselves, *Can we create a setting that could have been the story behind each of the parables to help children and parents connect better with them?*

Tales That Teach is the result of our attempts to answer those questions while prayerfully seeking to remain true to the lessons and the details in the Bible. Please note that in some cases we revised the parables for young children by removing elements of the original that could cause them anxiety and stress.

As you read together and bring your children to Jesus for His blessing, we hope everyone in your family will prayerfully ask and discuss, "What is the teaching Jesus wants us to learn from this story? What is His kingdom like? How can I accept God's invitation to be a part of His kingdom?"

Each story includes Bible study tools. We suggest that you begin by praying together and then explore the following:

- A Bible verse for your children to learn that focuses on one of the lessons of the story.

- Information about where to find the original parable in the Bible so you and your children can read it together and talk about what Jesus was trying to teach.

- Information about where to find a similar story or Bible verse that talks about the same subject so you and your children can compare the scriptures.

- Questions to ponder and discuss with your children to encourage them to think and talk with you about their Bible learning.

- Projects for parents and children to work on together to better connect with and apply the story's lesson. Provide journals for your children because some of the activities suggest your children write or draw journal entries.

We hope these stories inspire a deeper study of the Bible. To that end, we share this promise from Jeremiah 29:13: "You will seek me and find me when you seek me with all your heart."

Two Builders, Two Houses

For no one can lay any foundation other than the one already laid, which is Jesus Christ.

—1 Corinthians 3:11

For thousands of years, God lived far away from the people He had created because sin had separated them from Him. Information about His creative power could be seen in nature (Romans 1:20). Stories about Him were passed down from parents to children. However, people started making assumptions about God that were not always accurate. And then, one day God arrived on Earth as a baby named Jesus. He came, in part, to clear up the confusion about who God is and what He is like.

Jesus was the *best* Storyteller ever. He often began His parable stories with the phrase "The kingdom of heaven is like . . . ," and then He would use something in nature or an experience from real life to teach a truth about God. It was a popular teaching method in those days. He knew not everyone would understand everything right away, but He left a seed planted in their hearts that would take root and grow as they remembered the story details.

Early in His ministry, Jesus preached on the side of a mountain to thousands of people. He told many parables that day, and He ended His sermon with one that went like the story that follows.

This chapter is based on Matthew 7:24–27; Luke 6:46–49; and Christ's Object Lessons, *chapter 1, "Teaching in Parables."*

* * * * *

Jared stretched his arms and legs under the bedcovers. The day to start building his own house had arrived at last. Silently, he dressed in the dark and put on his shoes. He headed to the toolshed where he grabbed a pair of gloves and the pickax. Jared knew his first and most important job would be to dig through the clay soil to get to the rock base. On that rock foundation, he would build the stone walls of his house.

The chittering of sparrows accompanied Jared's climb up the hill to the property he had purchased the previous fall. The sun rose over the eastern shore of the lake in the valley below as he carefully paced out the perimeter of the house, placing markers at the corners to guide him as he dug through the soil. Then he put his muscles and the pickax to work.

By noon, Jared had exposed the rock in only two square feet—five inches deep—in one corner of the foundation area. Sweat soaked his clothes when he stopped to rest and eat his meal of cheese and bread.

I knew it would be hard work to clear away the clay, he thought as he chewed on the bread, *but I didn't realize the progress would be so slow. This clay feels as hard as rock!*

Halfway around the hill and much closer to the lake, another young man swung a pickax. John had started building his house the week before, after pacing out the perimeter of the foundation. Today he continued to dig away at the clay soil to find the rock beneath.

This is ridiculous! I've been working on digging down to the rock for over a week with very little reward for my efforts, he thought. *The man I bought the property from warned me the bedrock might be several feet down this close to the lake. Well, this clay sure seems as hard as rock. Hey! That gives me an idea.*

* * * * *

John and his wife moved into their house in midsummer. Mud held the rock walls together, and a strong roof provided shelter from the hot, sunny days. John anchored his fishing boat near the shore and enjoyed the view of the lake while he ate his supper each evening.

Jared struggled to finish the walls on his house before the end of summer and celebrated with his family when the last nail was hammered into the roof a few weeks later. He rested peacefully when he heard the *drip, drip, drip* of rain one night, signaling the beginning of the rainy season. In the morning, Jared checked the walls where they met the bedrock. The walls were secure. When the rain began to pour from the sky and rivulets of water flowed around his house, the walls remained unmoved.

Summary

Making the teachings of Jesus the reason for all our decisions in life helps us to find happiness forever.

John, on the other hand, faced a crisis. The rivulets of water flowing by his home started eating away at the clay he had failed to remove before building the walls of the house. When the water started running through the center of the bedroom, he begged friends to let him and his wife stay at their house. When he could return to check on the building, the front wall had collapsed, along with the roof. The rain continued to fall for weeks, and by the time the rainy season was over, no walls were standing.

"I should have put in the time to dig down to the bedrock," he apologized to his wife. "Now everything is ruined. Forgive me for not focusing on the foundation—the most important part."

* * * * *

"Build your life on the foundation of My teachings," Jesus told His listeners. "It's the only way your life will be secure."

Teaching Tips

1. Read the original parable in Matthew 7:24–27 and Luke 6:46–49. What do these stories help you understand about Jesus?

2. What is it like to hear and follow the teachings of Jesus?

3. What "hard clay" have you had to dig through to build your friendship with Jesus?

4. Ask your children to think about a time when they were given instructions to follow and failed to follow them. Then ask your children to think about a time when they did follow instructions. Share similar stories from your own life with your children. How are your stories like the stories of the wise and foolish builders?

5. Work with your children to start a journal, and list (in words or drawings) the teachings of Jesus. Add to the list as you learn more about what Jesus taught.

Planting Time

Sarah ran down the path to meet her father as he returned from working in the barley field, calling, "Abba [Father]!"

Benjamin, Sarah's father, scooped up his child and hoisted her onto his shoulders for the short walk to their yard. "How is my precious girl? You were still sleeping when I left this morning."

"I'm happy today!" Sarah replied. "I helped Ima [Mother]."

"How did you help her?"

"I chased birds," chirped Sarah.

"Why did you chase birds?" Benjamin asked as he set her on the ground.

"I chased them away from the garden!" Sarah's lilting voice sounded surprised that he would need to ask.

"Oh, I see. How many birds did you scare away?"

This chapter is based on Matthew 13:1–9, 18–23; Mark 4:1–20; Luke 8:4–15; and Christ's Object Lessons, chapter 2, " 'The Sower Went Forth to Sow.' "

Scripture

And without faith it is impossible to please God, because anyone who comes to him must believe that he exists and that he rewards those who earnestly seek him.

—Hebrews 11:6

"One hundred and two ninety," she replied, holding up all the fingers on both of her hands.

"That's a lot of birds."

"Yes. I'm a good bird chaser!"

Smiling, Eva, Sarah's mother, joined them in the front yard. "Welcome home, Benjamin. How did the barley planting go today?"

"I'm thankful for the early rains. They have softened the soil so I was able to finish plowing the east end of the field. Tomorrow I will scatter the seeds for that section."

"You made good progress!" Eva complimented.

"Sarah tells me she was a bird chaser today."

"Indeed, she was! She kept the crows away from the cucumber seeds until I could cover them with soil," explained Eva.

"Those bad birds tried to steal seeds, but I made them go away!" Sarah looked satisfied with her success.

"You know, Sarah, you could help me when I plant the barley tomorrow. Sometimes birds try to steal the barley seeds too."

"Can I help Abba tomorrow?" Sarah looked pleadingly at Eva.

"How about you and I take lunch to Abba tomorrow, and you can help him then?" Eva asked.

Sarah danced with happiness at the thought.

In the morning, Sarah woke up early but not early enough to see her abba before he left for the field. She played with the wooden goat her abba had carved while Eva packed a meal of cheese, olives, and bread to take to Benjamin at midmorning.

When they arrived at the east end of their field, Eva and Sarah saw Benjamin with a bag slung over his shoulder. They watched as he reached into the sack for a handful of seeds and then threw his arm in a wide arc with his hand open to scatter them in the furrows he had plowed the day before.

Sarah and Eva waved in greeting when Benjamin looked up from his work. He took the bag off of his shoulder and crossed the field to meet them.

"How are my two beautiful girls doing?" he asked as he picked up Sarah and then hugged both of them at the same time.

Sarah giggled. "We bringed you a 'licious lunch, Abba!"

"I can hardly wait to share it with you," he laughed.

The three of them settled under the shade of an olive

tree, gave thanks to God for the food, and began to eat. Well, Eva and Benjamin ate. When Sarah opened her eyes from the prayer, she saw a flock of crows landing on the edge of the field a short distance away.

"Bad birds!" she yelled as she ran toward them. They flew off, and Sarah happily returned to the lunch. "I'm a good bird chaser!"

Sarah's meal was interrupted several more times as she faithfully chased the crows away from the seeds.

Before Eva and Sarah left to go home, Benjamin gave them a tour of the field. He carried Sarah on his shoulders—a place she loved to be.

The seeds he had planted two weeks earlier had germinated, and the stalks and leaves stood a few inches tall. He pointed out the growth. "See those plants over there by the rocks?" he asked Sarah. "They have a good start, but the rocks will make it difficult for the barley plants to keep growing when it gets hot. They won't get enough water because their roots don't go very deep."

"See the big plants, Abba?"

"Yes, I see them, Sarah. Unfortunately, those big plants are weeds. If you look closely, you'll see the seeds I planted are growing in the middle of them. More than likely, the weeds will choke out the barley."

"Bad weeds!" said Sarah.

"Look over there, though." He pointed to the middle of the field. "The seeds that fell into the good soil will provide a good harvest and plenty of food for our family and others."

"May God bless your labors, Benjamin," Eva said and then squeezed his hand. "Well, Sarah, we better go back home. There might be more birds for you to chase away from the garden."

"OK. Bye-bye, Abba. See you later!"

Benjamin set Sarah on the ground. "OK, Sarah. I'm glad Ima has you to help her! See you tonight!"

Just before Sarah and Eva turned up the path toward their house, they turned to wave once more. But Benjamin didn't notice. With the seed sack slung back over his shoulder, he had already begun to scatter more barley seeds.

Teaching Tips

1. The parable of the sower is found in Matthew 13:1–9, 18–23; Mark 4:1–20; and Luke 8:4–15. Help your children make a list of the differences and similarities between these versions of the story in their journals.

2. Why did Jesus use the story of the sower to explain God's kingdom?

3. Who does the farmer in the story represent?

4. Work with your children to draw pictures in their journals that tells the story of the sower. Be sure to include all of the places where the seeds landed and what happened to the seeds in those places.

5. Be very specific with the pictures in their journals, and discuss what kinds of things in your lives are like the birds, thorns, and rocky soil. Pray together to ask Jesus for a heart that is like the good soil in the parable.

Summary

We receive forgiveness and love when we believe God's Word and our hearts sincerely want to know the truth about Jesus.

Sarah's Question

Scripture

I will give you a new heart and put a new spirit in you; I will remove from you your heart of stone and give you a heart of flesh.

—Ezekiel 36:26

A few weeks later, Sarah and Ima again decided to take lunch to Benjamin in the barley field. "Hurry, Ima! Abba will be hungry for his lunch!" Sarah insisted.

"I'm hurrying, Sarah. I'm almost finished with the special fig cake for Abba. I just need a few more minutes."

Sarah danced at the doorway in excitement. She loved spending time with Abba, and today she had an important question to ask him.

"Ready?" Ima asked.

"Ready!"

"Do you think you can carry the basket with the carrots and cucumbers?" Ima asked.

"Yes! I will carry it very carefully." Sarah put her arm under the basket's handle and showed Ima how she would balance it so the contents wouldn't spill.

"That's a good plan, Sarah."

This chapter is based on Mark 4:26–29 and Christ's Object Lessons, *chapter 3, " 'First the Blade, Then the Ear.' "*

They headed out the door and down the path toward the barley field. The sun warmed their backs just enough, and they joined the warble of the birds with their own song of praise.

Benjamin saw them headed his way and waved a greeting from across the field. Sarah handed her basket to Ima and took off running toward Abba. He caught her up in his arms and swung her high above his head. Sarah giggled in delight.

"We bringed you a 'licious lunch again, Abba."

"Thank you! I am so hungry! Looks like Ima has chosen to sit under that olive tree close to the path. I'll race you to her," Benjamin challenged.

"Ready, set, go!" called out Sarah. She started running the second her feet touched the ground.

"Hey, wait for me!" Benjamin followed in protest.

They both reached Eva at the same time. "I call it a tie!" she exclaimed, laughing, as Benjamin and Sarah collapsed on the ground in front of her.

First, Sarah chattered about their morning while they ate. But before they finished, Sarah asked the question she had been wondering about all day. "Abba, how do you make the barley grow?"

"Well, Sarah, I don't make it grow."

"You planted the seeds."

"Yes, I planted the seeds, but the rest of the growing is a miracle from God."

"A *mir-cle?*"

"Yes, a miracle. It's something that happens because of the power of our God, who loves us very much. I planted the seeds. He sends the rain to water the seeds and the sun to help warm them so they can grow."

Benjamin pulled up a barley stalk that grew nearby. "Do you see these roots? They grow down into the soil. The stalk grows up toward the sun with leaves that catch its warmth. Soon the barley grain grows."

"But how?" Sarah wanted to know.

"I trust God to make it grow, Sarah. I throw the seed onto the ground, and whether I am sleeping or awake, God does the rest. That's the miracle."

Sarah stood up tall. "See? I'm growing bigger. Is that a mir-cle too?"

"It surely is," Abba replied. "God grows you and our food!"

"Fig cake, anyone?" Eva asked.

Summary

Just like God makes plants grow, His love will grow in our hearts if we ask Him.

"I need two pieces, Ima, because God is growing me bigger!" Sarah looked hopeful.

Benjamin and Eva grinned. "Maybe next time, sweet Sarah. Maybe next time."

Teaching Tips

1. Compare this parable found in Mark 4:26–29 with Isaiah 61:11, which promises that God will cause "righteousness and praise" to grow. What do these verses help you understand about God's power?

2. What do seeds need to be able to germinate and grow?

3. What do people need to have a growing friendship with Jesus?

4. Buy some bean seeds. Place two or three seeds between two paper towels that have been folded and place them inside a plastic bag. Tape the plastic bag to a window that receives lots of sunshine. Keep the paper towels moist by adding some water every day. Watch the seeds germinate and grow. Wonder with your children about how God makes plants grow, and thank Him for the miracle of food.

5. Share how God has grown His love in your heart, and ask your children to tell their stories too.

Wheat Porridge With Honey

One evening Benjamin, Eva, and Sarah lingered at the supper table. The light from the orange-and-pink sunset filled their home. It brought the day's work to an end and bathed their quiet conversation after the evening meal with peace.

"How is the wheat in the north field doing?" Eva asked Benjamin.

"Ima, what is *wheat*?" Sarah asked.

"Wheat is what I use to make porridge sometimes. You like to eat it for breakfast with honey," Ima replied.

"Oh, yes, I like porridge and honey," Sarah added.

"I'm glad you do, Sarah, because a large amount of wheat is growing in the north field this year. You should be able to eat lots of porridge and honey after the harvest," Abba explained. "The plants are looking healthy, and the wheat berries should appear any day now."

"Maybe tomorrow, Abba?" Sarah asked with a yawn.

"Maybe tomorrow," Abba replied.

This chapter is based on Matthew 13:24–30, 37–43 and Christ's Object Lessons, *chapter 4, "Tares."*

Scripture

The Lord is not slow in keeping his promise, as some understand slowness. Instead he is patient with you, not wanting anyone to perish, but everyone to come to repentance.

—2 Peter 3:9

"Time for you to be in bed, sweet Sarah. Give Abba a hug good night, and then I'll help you get ready to sleep," Ima said.

"See you tomorrow when I return from the fields. Dream of eating porridge and honey so you have a sweet sleep!" Abba laughed.

Sarah giggled and trotted to her room, following Ima.

* * * * *

As she usually did, Sarah waited for her abba in front of the house the next day. She ran to meet him when he walked up the path to their home.

"How is the wheat today, Abba? Will I be able to eat porridge soon?" Sarah asked.

"I thought you might ask about that." Benjamin smiled at Sarah. "I'll tell you what I saw while we eat supper tonight. Let's see if Ima has everything ready for us."

"Welcome home, Benjamin," Eva greeted him with a hug. "Sarah, thank you for bringing Abba inside so quickly. Supper is ready."

Benjamin thanked God for the lentils and barley bread Eva had prepared, and Sarah ended the blessing with a cheerful "Amen!"

"How is the wheat today, Abba?" Sarah asked again.

"Well, today I saw wheat berries starting to form on the top of the wheat plants," Abba responded

"Great news!" said Eva.

"But I also saw poisonous weeds growing with the wheat," Benjamin added.

"But that can't be right," objected Eva. "You didn't plant weed seeds with the wheat seeds."

Benjamin continued, "I can't think who would do this to us, but my helpers think that someone who wants to hurt our harvest scattered the weed seeds a night or two after I planted the wheat. Whoever it was planted the kind of weeds that look exactly like wheat plants right up until the wheat berries start appearing."

"Bad weeds! Did our *em-en-y* plant those weeds, Abba?" Sarah asked.

"How do you know the word *enemy*, Sarah?" Eva asked.

"Abba tells me stories about the *em-en-ies* of Israel— like the *Phil-steens*," Sarah explained

"That's true. I have told you stories about the Philistines," Benjamin agreed.

"I know! Pull up the weeds, Abba! Then they won't hurt the wheat!" Sarah suggested.

"That's what my helpers suggested as well. Unfortunately, it's not that simple. When the weeds and the wheat grow together, their roots grow together too. If the weeds are pulled, some of the wheat would also get pulled," Benjamin said thoughtfully.

"What will you do?" Eva asked.

"We'll wait for the harvesttime," explained Benjamin. "The weeds will go into one pile and the wheat into another."

"And then Ima can make me porridge?" Sarah asked.

"Yes, Sarah, then you can enjoy the wheat porridge you love," Abba agreed.

"With honey?" Sarah added eagerly.

"Yes, with honey!" Ima smiled.

Summary

Jesus is a wise caretaker, who has compassion for everyone.

Teaching Tips

1. Find this story in Matthew 13:24–30 and Jesus' explanation in Matthew 13:36–43. What does this story teach you about the enemy of God's kingdom?

2. Who is the sower of the good seeds, and what do the good seeds represent?

3. Compare the story of the weeds with 2 Peter 3:9, where Peter explains why God is not slow in keeping His promise to return.

4. Work with your children, and pull weeds in a garden or a lawn where the roots of the weeds grow close to the roots of good plants. Observe and discuss what happens when the weeds are pulled.

5. List some of the things in life that would be considered "weed seeds." Then discuss how to keep the enemy from planting "weed seeds" in your life. Ask your children to write or draw some of these ideas in their journals.

Teeny, Tiny Seeds

"Sarah, I have something to show you," called Abba one afternoon as he walked into the house.

Curious, Sarah placed the wooden goat she had been playing with into its tree-twig corral and sat next to her abba at the table. "What do you have, Abba?"

"I have some seeds. I thought it would be fun for you to try to guess the plants that will grow from them."

"That's like a game, Abba! I like to play games!"

"Me too!"

Eva walked over to the table where they sat. "May I join your game?"

"Yes, Ima! Sit by me," insisted Sarah.

Benjamin pulled a seed from his pocket and placed it on the table. "Here's the first seed. What do you see?"

"It's brown," answered Sarah.

This chapter is based on Matthew 13:31, 32; Mark 4:30–32; Luke 13:18, 19; and Christ's Object Lessons, chapter 5, " 'Like a Grain of Mustard Seed.' "

Scripture

He said to them, "Go into all the world and preach the gospel [good news] to all creation."

—Mark 16:15

"What else do you see?" Benjamin asked.

"It has a line down the middle. And it's like a small, long circle."

"That long circle is called an oval," explained Eva.

"Good details to notice," said Benjamin. "What do you think grows from this seed?"

"I don't know," Sarah said as she looked at her abba questioningly.

"I do!" Eva said. "That looks like a wheat seed."

"You are right!"

"My wheat porridge doesn't look like that!" Sarah said.

"That's because Ima grinds the wheat seeds before she makes the porridge."

Benjamin placed a second seed on the table. "Here's the next seed. Describe what you see."

Sarah looked carefully. "It's brown. It's like a pointy wheat seed."

"Do you know what grows from this seed?" Benjamin asked.

"Cucumbers?" Sarah suggested.

"Why do you think cucumbers?" Eva asked.

"Because cucumbers are pointy on the ends."

"*Hmm*. That's an interesting idea. However, did you know that how the seed looks isn't the way the full-grown plant or fruit looks?" Benjamin asked.

"Why not?"

"Because God hides what the plant will be like inside the seed. However, we can be sure that a wheat seed will grow wheat. A cucumber seed will grow cucumbers."

"Then I can't see what plant is in this seed because it's hiding." Sarah pointed to the small, pointy brown seed on the table.

"I'll give you a hint. You chased the crows away from eating this kind of seed," Abba said.

"It's a barley seed!" she announced happily. Then she reminded her parents, "I'm a good bird chaser!"

"Yes, you are," agreed Ima.

"Ima, can we eat barley bread for supper tonight?"

"I have some ready and waiting."

Abba dug into his other pocket to find the seeds he had gathered on his way home the day before. He placed five or six of them on the table for Sarah to examine. "Here are the last seeds for today."

"Teeny, tiny seeds," exclaimed Sarah. "Oh, they are so cute! Are those seeds for teeny, tiny flowers?"

"Those are seeds from something that grows close enough to see from the front of our house. Come outside with me, and I will show you," Benjamin invited.

They followed him out the door. Sarah ran over to some small pink flowers growing by the garden. "Do those seeds grow pink flowers?"

"Not pink flowers," answered Eva.

Sarah looked all around, then pointed to the white flowers by the door of their home. "Those?" she asked.

"No, not those either," replied Benjamin. "Stand by me, and I'll show you what grows from the teeny, tiny seeds." He crouched down so his face was at the same level as hers. Then he pointed to their neighbor's house to the south. "Do you see that tree growing in our neighbor's field? That mustard tree grew from one of these seeds."

"But that's a big tree," she objected, "and those are teeny, tiny seeds!"

"If we let God work, He can grow big things from teeny, tiny seeds."

Sarah's eyebrows scrunched together as she tried to understand. Eva picked her up and gave her a hug. "Abba and I are planting a seed of love for God in your heart. Will you let God grow it inside of you?"

Sarah's face relaxed into a smile as she looked into her ima's eyes, and she whispered, "Yes."

Teaching Tips

1. This parable is found in the Bible in three places: Matthew 13:31, 32; Mark 4:30–32; and Luke 13:18, 19. Read and compare these passages to find how they are the same and how they are different.

2. What does the mustard seed represent?

3. Why is it important that the mustard tree grows large enough to allow birds to rest in its branches?

4. Purchase or collect seeds of different types. Play the seed game like Sarah and her abba did. Look at real plants or pictures of the plants that grow from each seed. Does the size of the seed "match" with the size of the plant?

5. Pray with your children, and ask Jesus to help you tell the good news about Him to someone this week. Ask your children to write or draw the story in their journals of what happened when they shared about Jesus with someone.

Summary

The kingdom of heaven has room for people from everywhere. We can practice being the followers of Jesus by welcoming everyone.

Sarah Helps the Cucumbers

Scripture

Remember this: Whoever sows sparingly will also reap sparingly, and whoever sows generously will also reap generously.

—2 Corinthians 9:6

"Those cucumbers we planted a few weeks ago need our help this morning. Would you like to work in the garden with me?" Ima asked Sarah while she dried her hands from washing the breakfast dishes.

Sarah looked up from where she was playing on the floor. "Has God growed me big enough to help, Ima?"

"I'm sure of it!" Ima smiled.

"Yes!" cheered Sarah.

"OK! Let's go outside to the shed where Abba keeps our tools. We'll need the hoe to clean away the weeds, some straw to mulch the cucumber hills, and a handful of seeds to start the next set of cucumber plants."

Sarah followed Ima to the shed, chattering to her about flowers and mustard trees, chasing crows and butterflies, and playing with her toy wooden goat and its tree-twig corral.

"I left some barley grits for my goat so he won't get hungry while I'm helping

This chapter is based on Christ's Object Lessons, *chapter 6, "Other Lessons From Seed-Sowing."*

you. I put some straw in his corral, in case he gets tired and wants to take a nap."

"Sounds like you are looking out for the needs of your goat," replied Ima.

At the shed, Ima took down the hoe from its place on the wall. Next, she put some cucumber seeds in a small cloth bag and handed it to Sarah. Then she found a bucket and filled it with straw.

"Lead us to the garden, Sarah. We have what we need to help our cucumber patch."

"Follow me! I know the way."

When they reached the garden, Sarah asked, "Which plants are the cucumbers, Ima?"

"Well, let's look at the cucumber seeds and see whether you can guess," suggested Ima.

"That won't work. God keeps the plants hidden inside the seeds. Remember what Abba said?"

"Do you want to see the seeds anyway?" Ima asked.

"Yes. Then when Abba and I play the seed game again, I will know the answer."

Ima opened the bag Sarah had carried to the garden. She placed three cucumber seeds onto the palm of her open hand. "What do you see?"

"They look flat and light brown and pointy. Hey, I remember eating seeds like this inside a cucumber! Why didn't we eat these seeds?"

"When we save some of the seeds instead of eating them all, we trust that God will help us grow more food," explained Ima. "And when we plant the seeds, God makes new life grow from them."

Sarah looked carefully around the garden and then asked again, "Which plants are the cucumber plants?"

"I'll describe them. See if you can figure it out," suggested Ima. "First, look for clusters of flat leaves that are the shape of your hand with your fingers spread open."

Sarah looked at her open hand and at the plants in the garden but asked for more clues. "What else?"

"Look for plants that are growing long vines that look like ropes."

Sarah looked but asked again, "What else?"

"Look for plants that are growing on small hills."

"I found them! I found them! The cucumber plants are over here!" Sarah ran to the corner of the garden where Ima had planted the cucumber seeds.

"You are right. Congratulations!" Ima carried the

hoe and the bucket of straw over to where Sarah stood.

"How do we help the cucumbers?"

"We need to get rid of the weeds around the plants," Ima replied.

"Bad weeds! They can choke the cucumbers."

"You remember the lesson Abba taught you in the barley field! I'll cut the weeds at the root with the hoe. You can collect the cut weeds and put them in a pile by the garden fence."

Ima and Sarah worked side by side, removing all the weeds they could see.

"Now we'll put straw on the cucumber hills. When we water the cucumbers, the straw will protect the plants from drying up too fast."

Sarah and Ima arranged the straw, then filled the bucket to water the cucumbers.

"Time to plant more cucumber seeds!" Ima announced. "First, I'll make the hills with the hoe."

Sarah watched, holding the bag of seeds.

"Bring the seeds," Ima called.

Sarah learned how to plant two or three seeds near the top of every hill. After the seeds were planted, they worked together to cover the hills with straw and water the seeds.

Sarah was unusually quiet while they rested in the shade and enjoyed looking at their work in the cucumber patch.

"What are you thinking about?" Ima asked.

"Can I help again tomorrow? I like working with God in our garden."

"For sure, sweet Sarah. Tomorrow let's help the mint plants."

Summary

When we share Jesus' love and compassion with others, our own blessings grow bigger.

Teaching Tips

1. Compare the phrase in 2 Corinthians 9:6 about sowing generously with the phrase in Galatians 6:7 about reaping what we sow. What do these verses help you understand about God's kingdom?

2. Compare the phrase in John 12:24 about a seed dying with the phrase in 1 Corinthians 15:42, 43 about resurrection. What does this help you understand about God's power to change the circumstances and lives of people?

3. How do people help God when they share His love?

4. Buy some cucumber seeds (or other seeds for plants that grow well in your area), and plant them in a garden or a large pot. Work with your children to care for the growing plants. Ask your children to draw pictures in their journals to document the miracle of growth God provides. Ask your children to share what they learn about God from watching the plants grow.

5. Think about ways to plant seeds of compassion this week.

Bigger, Lighter, and Tastier

Tabitha was sitting in her kitchen, thinking about her plans for the next day. She stood up to look in the cupboard. *We don't have enough bread left for supper tomorrow. It's time to bake some more.*

She called to her children, Jesse and Rachel. "We need to bake some bread, and I thought it would be fun if we did it together. If we start tonight, we will ensure that the bread will be ready for supper tomorrow."

"I would love to learn how to make bread," Rachel said.

"What do we need to do first?" Jesse asked.

"We have to grind the wheat," Tabitha told her children. They took the cover off the big jar that held the kernels of wheat. Jesse found the flat stones that were used to grind the grain. Rachel put some of the kernels between the stones, and Jesse rubbed them together in a circular motion. When he was tired, Rachel took a turn. Soon there was a little pile of soft beige wheat flour. Grinding enough wheat for the bread took a long time.

This chapter is based on Matthew 13:33; Luke 13:20, 21; and Christ's Object Lessons, *chapter 7, "Like Unto Leaven."*

Scripture

Sanctify them by the truth; your word is truth.

—John 17:17

When they were finished grinding, their mother put the flour in a dough trough, then added water, salt, and leavening. "Why did you put in some leftover bread dough?" Rachel asked.

"It's called leavening, which is similar to yeast. It makes the dough rise or become bigger. The bread is lighter and easier to eat and digest. Without leavening, the bread would be flat and very heavy," Tabitha explained. "We will mix the dough all together and knead it."

"What does *knead* mean?" Jesse asked.

"You'll see in just a minute," Tabitha said.

"I know how." Rachel asked, "Can I help you knead?"

"Yes, you may," answered their mother as she spread the dough onto a flour-dusted table. With flour on her hands, she made a mound of dough and pushed it down with the heel of her hand (the raised part of her palm close to her wrist). She turned the dough partially around and pushed it down with the heel of her hand again. Jesse and Rachel each made a mound of dough and repeated their mother's actions. Together they kneaded the dough for about ten minutes. Then they put the dough in the dough trough. Tabitha covered it with a kitchen towel, and they left it to rise.

In the morning, Rachel hurried into the kitchen to check on the bread dough. She was so surprised to see how much the dough had risen. "Ima, Jesse, come quick! Our bread dough looks so different from how it did last night."

Jesse and their mother hurried at Rachel's call. "Look, Ima. We have twice as much dough as we did last night. Is that because of the leavening?" he asked.

"You're right. The leavening has made the dough rise. Now we have to punch it down and let it rise again. This time it will rise much more quickly," Tabitha explained.

When the dough had risen again, the three made it into loaves and baked it in a clay oven. The freshly baked bread smelled delicious.

"Please, Ima, may we eat some of it?" Jesse begged when the bread came out of the oven.

"Please, Ima, please," begged Rachel.

"Yes, it does taste best as soon as it's cool enough to eat," Tabitha agreed. "You may each have a piece. We'll save the rest for supper. What have you learned about bread making?"

Summary

Yeast, or leavening, changes bread dough like listening to Jesus changes us.

"The leavening changes the bread, making it bigger, lighter, and tastier," Rachel said.

"That's true," said Jesse. "Making bread is complicated. The flour, the salt, and the water are changed by the leavening into something delicious."

Teaching Tips

1. Find the original parable in Matthew 13:33 and Luke 13:20, 21. How are these two versions of the parable similar, and how are they different?

2. Does the flour in the bread dough work hard to be changed? Why, or why not?

3. How would the bread be different if it was made without yeast?

4. How does God make His kingdom grow in our lives?

5. Work with your children to make some yeast bread. Share the results with your family, and explain the story Jesus told about yeast.

Note: In the story, Tabitha used a method of bread making called leavening. This method is still used today in making sourdough bread. It works by keeping some dough from the last time bread was made and adding it to the new batch to make it rise. Another method of bread making uses yeast, which is added to the other ingredients to make it rise.

Nathan's Treasure

Scripture

If you look for it as for silver and search for it as for hidden treasure, then you will understand the fear of the LORD and find the knowledge of God.

—Proverbs 2:4, 5

Nathan followed his ox and plow on this land along the river. He had just rented a field that had not been planted for several years. He and the ox had a hard job because there were lots of weeds. As he neared the end of a row, Nathan felt the plow pull against something solid. *I wonder what that is.*

Nathan dug around whatever had caught his plow. Imagine his surprise when he found a heavy metal box. He stooped to pick it up. Something shiny stuck out from the box. Opening it, he was astonished to find gold coins. He hid one of the coins in his belt, thinking he could ask Uncle Josiah about its value. Then, looking around, Nathan saw that he was alone and quickly put the box back in the hole, covered it with dirt, and stomped over it to hide the hole. *These coins might be really valuable. I must keep them hidden.*

Nathan hurried down the trail to town, leading the ox and plow. When he reached the town gate, he found many older men sitting together, chatting as they usually did.

"How much would it cost to buy that fallow field by the river? Rachel and I are

This chapter is based on Matthew 13:44 and Christ's Object Lessons, *chapter 8, "Hidden Treasure."*

planning to marry in a few months. Do you think I could build a new house on that property for us to live in?" Nathan asked the group.

"Why would you want to do that? Your dad is already planning a new room for the family house. I promised I would help build it," Uncle Josiah told Nathan. "Come on; it's time for lunch. Your mom will have something good for us to eat."

As the two walked home together, Nathan took the coin from its hiding place and asked Uncle Josiah, "Have you ever seen anything like this before? Please don't tell anyone about it. It's a secret."

Uncle Josiah took the coin from Nathan. He bit it. "It's real gold," he told his nephew.

"It looks like an old Babylonian coin. It must be worth a lot. Is there more than one coin?"

"Yes, there are quite a number. How can I find its value?" Nathan asked.

"You can go to the market in the next town and ask the money changers. Of course, you must be very vague about where you found it," Uncle Josiah said. "What will you do if the coin is valuable?"

"If I can buy the old farm, the coins will be mine," Nathan said.

"After lunch, your father could ask about the value of that field," Uncle Josiah said as they sat down to eat.

"Whatever are you talking about?" Benjamin, Nathan's father, asked.

"I found some old coins in the field I rented near the river. Uncle Josiah thinks the coins are valuable gold Babylonian coins," Nathan told his dad.

That afternoon Nathan discovered that the old coins were a real treasure—worth far more than the field. Meanwhile, Benjamin and his brother, Josiah, talked to several people in the village to determine the value of the property. The owner was Judith, a widow who lived in the village.

Josiah and Benjamin didn't want to act too interested, but they did ask the old lady if she wanted to sell it.

When Nathan came back from the market in the next town, he was very excited.

"Does Judith want to sell the field?" Nathan asked his father and uncle. "Did she say how much the price might be?"

Benjamin and Uncle Josiah shared the amount Judith wanted for the land.

Nathan told them the value of the coins and how

many there were. "I must buy the field," Nathan insisted. "I will sell everything I have. I will do any work available, but I must buy the field."

"You must explain your actions to Rachel, or she will think that you have gone crazy," Benjamin told him, and Uncle Josiah agreed.

"I'm not worried—Rachel trusts me. Everyone else in town may think that I'm crazy, but I don't care," Nathan insisted.

Nathan sold his favorite donkey and found some extra work to make more money. Rachel sold some of her jewelry. Benjamin and Uncle Josiah both lent Nathan some money. When he finally had enough money, Nathan bought the field from Judith.

Soon after, Rachel walked with him to the field where they dug up the treasure box. She opened the box, running her fingers through the gold coins. They repaid Nathan's father and uncle the money they had borrowed and built a new house on the edge of their field.

Teaching Tips

1. Read Jesus' story in Matthew 13:44.
2. Read a similar story in the next two verses: Matthew 13:45, 46. What are the similarities and differences in the two stories?
3. What does it mean that Nathan sold everything to buy the field?
4. What does the treasure represent?
5. Does your family have a treasured item? Who takes care of it, and where is it? What makes it special? Make up your own parable to explain the kingdom of heaven using your family's treasure.

Summary

The Bible is like a treasure chest, full of information about Jesus and His love for us.

The Pearl

One day Jesus and His disciples walked through the market area in Jerusalem. So many interesting things were for sale. Peter inspected the fish, commenting to James, "These fish don't look as fresh as ones we catch in the Sea of Galilee."

Thomas looked hungrily at the beautiful grapes. "These grapes look delicious! Should we get some for our supper?"

Judas noticed the sellers of gems and pearls. "Look at that merchant. He's admiring a spectacular pearl!"

The others turned to look at the pearl buyer. As he cradled the large, lustrous pearl in his hand, he asked the shop owner, "How much is this pearl?"

"That pearl is very special. It's the most valuable one that I have. I would be happy to keep it myself. Make me an offer, and I'll consider it," the shopkeeper answered.

The pearl buyer looked at it once more, shook his head, and returned it to the

This chapter is based on Matthew 13:45, 46 and Christ's Object Lessons, *chapter 9, "The Pearl."*

shelf where the shop owner had displayed it with obvious care. He turned and walked away.

The disciples said to each other, "I thought that he would buy it."

"Me too. His robe is made of fine material."

"He looks rich enough to buy such a beautiful pearl."

Right then, a mother brought her little boy to Jesus and asked Him to heal her child, who looked feverish and weak. Jesus took the child in His arms and touched his forehead. The child sat up and began looking around. Jesus set him down, and the boy hurried off to play.

Then Jesus and the disciples walked to another part of the city. A crowd followed them, so Jesus sat down to tell them some parables.

"Sometimes I just don't know what He means," Andrew whispered to his brother, Peter.

However, the next story caught their attention. "Again, the kingdom of heaven is like a merchant looking for fine pearls. When he found one of great value, he went away and sold everything he had and bought it" (Matthew 13:45, 46).

"Could that be the man we saw at the market?" the disciples quietly asked each other.

When Jesus had finished telling stories, He and the disciples walked back through the market to the place where they were staying. At the market, they recognized the man who had looked at the fabulous pearl. He had a bag and was showing its contents to the shop owner. The two men shook hands. The owner took the bag and gave the pearl to his customer.

"Just like Jesus' story," someone said.

That evening as they ate the food that they had bought at the market, Peter asked, "Jesus, what does the pearl story mean?"

"What do you think it means?" Jesus returned the question.

"Nothing is as important as following You?" Andrew suggested.

"You are right. You left your fishing boats and tax collector's booth to follow Me," Jesus said. "But the story also has another meaning."

"Another meaning?" they all asked. "How can it have another meaning?"

"It's something about Me. In another way, I am the merchant looking for a gorgeous pearl," Jesus said.

Summary

Finding Jesus is the most important thing in our lives. Finding people is the most important thing to Jesus.

"How can You be a merchant?" Peter asked.

"Does it mean that You are the man looking for pearls?" John wondered. "You have given all to find us?"

"Both meanings are correct," Jesus said. "Finding God's kingdom is more important than anything else in life. Also, finding you is the most important thing to Me."

"See, Peter. Jesus always has a deeper meaning than we imagine," Andrew said.

"I'm glad that He tells us the meaning of His stories," Peter answered. "Otherwise, I would never figure them out."

Teaching Tips

1. Find this parable in Matthew 13:45, 46. How is this story like the story of the lost coin in Luke 15:8–10?

2. Why is the merchant willing to sell all he has to buy the pearl?

3. How valuable to you is following Jesus? What treasured possession would you be willing to give up to have Jesus as King of your life?

4. If the pearl represents us and Jesus is the merchant, what does that say about how important you are to Jesus?

5. Zephaniah 3:17 says, "The Lord your God is with you, the Mighty Warrior who saves. He will take great delight in you; in his love he will no longer rebuke you, but will rejoice over you with singing." Work with your children to find or make up a song about Jesus' love. Practice it and sing it for family worship or share it with a friend.

Becoming a Fisherman

"Tobias, this is the day—the day you've been waiting for," Ezra, his father, said.

"Yes, Abba, I can hardly wait. Today I become a fisherman, just like you."

"It will be tonight. You must take a nap this afternoon so you'll be wide awake for our fishing expedition," Ezra told him.

"Abba, why do we fish at night?" Tobias asked.

"My son, the water in the Sea of Galilee is so clear that the fish can see our nets and swim away in the daytime. We fish at night so the fish can't see the nets."

That evening the two walked to the Sea of Galilee, carrying the food packed by Tobias's mom. At the shore, they met Asher, Ezra's brother, and Asher's son, Noam. The brothers fished together.

"Hey, Tobias, are you coming with us tonight?" his uncle asked. "We'll teach you to be a great fisherman."

The men took their nets and pushed their boats into the water. Tobias hopped into his abba's boat. When the two boats were far out in the lake, the fathers

This chapter is based on Matthew 13:47–50 and Christ's Object Lessons, *chapter 10, "The Net."*

tossed their largest net, fastening one side to each boat. The fathers told the two boys, "Make lots of noise to scare the fish into the net. Then we'll throw this lighter net over the bigger net and the fish to keep them from jumping out."

When the nets seemed to be full of fish, Ezra and Asher started rowing back to shore.

"Hey, you guys, the nets are really heavy. Come help us row," Ezra called to Tobias and Noam.

The boys helped row, but still the rowing was difficult as the nets were heavy with fish. Later, they noticed the sky in the east growing red as they reached the shore. The brothers jumped into the water to pull the nets out of the water, then the boys rowed the boats up to the sand and helped pull the boats ashore. "Will you bring the baskets over here by the nets?" Asher asked the boys.

Tobias and Noam followed his instructions and observed him.

"These fish are called tilapia. They are good for Jews to eat because they have fins and scales. Throw them in that first basket," said Asher.

"Yes, they're the ones we'll sell at the market," said Ezra. "See, this one looks like it has whiskers. It's called a catfish. We Jews don't eat them because they don't have fins and scales. But the Greeks who live on the other side of the lake like them, so we'll sell them there."

"These smaller fish are sardines. Your mothers will pickle them to preserve them to eat later," Asher said. "Put them in the third basket."

"What about these bigger fish?" Tobias asked.

"They're called carp. We'll sell them at the market too," Ezra explained.

"Everything else needs to be thrown back into the lake," Asher instructed the boys.

The sun was shining brightly when the contents of the nets were all sorted. Tobias and his cousin were ready to go home to breakfast and bed.

"I know you're tired, but first, we must take all the fish to the market and sell them. Then it's time to eat and sleep."

"I didn't know that being a fisherman was such hard work, Abba," Tobias said to his father.

"You'll get used to it. I was so tired when my abba first took me fishing. Now it's easy."

As they walked into the market with their baskets, customers hurried over to buy their fresh fish.

Summary

Jesus invites everyone to follow Him. We are free to make our own choice.

Teaching Tips

1. Find this parable in Matthew 13:47, 48. What does this parable teach about God's kingdom?

2. When do the fishermen sort the fish?

3. What other parables of Jesus teach the same lesson?

4. Why did Jesus tell stories about fish and fishermen?

5. In Matthew 4:18–20, Jesus invites Peter and Andrew to follow Him, and promises them they would "fish for people" (Matthew 4:19). Ask your children to write or draw in their journals to explain the meaning of fishing for people.

A Visitor at Night

Let me introduce myself. I am Nicodemus, a Pharisee and an important teacher of my people. I have seen Jesus heal people. I have heard Him preach. He is different from any of the other rabbis. Maybe He could even be the promised Messiah. I wanted to meet Him and talk to Him.

People said that He slept on the Mount of Olives, so one dark evening, I walked there alone, praying that God would help me find Jesus. I found Him sitting under a tree. Even though it was dark, I could see His eyes shining with kindness and love. I sat down beside Him and tried to ask diplomatically the questions I had been thinking about.

"Rabbi, we know that you are a teacher who has come from God. For no one could perform the signs you are doing if God were not with him" (John 3:2).

Jesus seemed to ignore the fact that I was trying to impress Him. "Very truly I tell you, no one can see the kingdom of God unless they are born again" (John 3:3).

"How can someone be born when they are old?" I asked (John 3:4).

This chapter is based on Matthew 13:51, 52 and Christ's Object Lessons, *chapter 11, "Things New and Old."*

Scripture

For God so loved the world that he gave his one and only Son, that whoever believes in him shall not perish but have eternal life.

—John 3:16

"Very truly I tell you, no one can enter the kingdom of God unless they are born of water and the Spirit. . . . 'You must be born again,' " Jesus answered (John 3:5, 7). "It's like the wind. You can't see the wind, but you can hear it and see what it does."

"What do you mean?" I asked.

"I've told you earthly things. How will you understand if I tell you heavenly things? Just as Moses lifted up the snake on the pole in the wilderness, I must be lifted up," Jesus answered.

"For God so loved the world that he gave his one and only Son, that whoever believes in him shall not perish but have eternal life. For God did not send his Son into the world to condemn the world, but to save the world through him," Jesus said (John 3:16, 17).

We talked a little longer. It almost seemed like Jesus could read my mind.

After my talk with Jesus, I studied the Scriptures. I prayed that God would show me if Jesus was the Messiah. I reread the story about Moses making the brass snake. When the people suffering from snakebites looked with faith at the brass snake Moses had put on a pole, they were healed. Jesus had said He would be lifted up like that serpent. I wondered what He meant.

At the time of the Feast of Tabernacles, Jesus came back to Jerusalem and preached in the temple. Many people thought that He was the Messiah—the Promised One. The jealous priests and leaders sent the temple guards to arrest Him.

When the guards returned without Jesus, they demanded, "Why didn't you arrest Him?"

"No one ever spoke like Jesus does. We couldn't arrest Him," the guards answered.

"Do you believe in Him also?" the priests asked angrily.

I stood up in the meeting and asked, "Does our law condemn a man without first hearing him to find out what he has been doing?" (John 7:51).

The priests and other Pharisees jeered at me. "Are you from Galilee, too? Look into it, and you will find that a prophet does not come out of Galilee" (John 7:52).

They made fun of me, but they didn't arrest Jesus. Well, they didn't arrest Him then.

At the time of Passover, Jesus rode a donkey into Jerusalem. The people called out, "Blessed is he who comes in the name of the LORD" (Psalm 118:26). On Thursday night, the priests and leaders did arrest

Jesus and tried Him. They judged Him guilty and condemned Him to death because they said He claimed that He was God's Son. They knew that I would object, so they didn't tell me about the meeting. The Roman governor, Pilate, condemned Jesus to be crucified with two thieves.

Like many, many others in Jerusalem, I walked through the crowded streets, going to Jesus' crucifixion. Arriving at the place of execution, I found a spot in the crowd where I could see Jesus' face. His appearance was changed. He was exhausted and in pain. But His eyes looked the same. Kindness and love shone from His eyes, just as when I had seen Him at the Mount of Olives.

"My God, my God, why have you forsaken me?" Jesus said (Psalm 22:1).

He was quoting a psalm. Lines from the rest of that psalm came to mind: "All who see me mock me; they hurl insults, shaking their heads" (Psalm 22:7).

I saw the priests and rulers yelling at Jesus, "You saved others; why don't You save Yourself? If You're the king of Israel, come down from the cross, and we will believe You."

Another passage from the psalm said, "They divide my clothes among them and cast lots for my garment" (Psalm 22:18). I saw the soldiers throwing dice to see who would get Jesus' clothes.

"My tongue sticks to the roof of my mouth," Jesus said (Psalm 22:15). Then I heard Jesus cry out, "I thirst."

Looking at Jesus on the cross, I saw the fulfillment of the psalm and remembered what He had said that night on the mount: "Just as Moses lifted up the snake, I must be lifted up." Now I understood. Jesus was lifted up on this hill so that I, and all other people who believe in Him, could have eternal life.

Jesus looked at me, and despite the tears that were rolling down my face, I saw love shining in His eyes.

"It is finished," Jesus said in a loud voice, and then He died (John 19:30).

The words Jesus said that night in the garden came back to my mind: "For God so loved." I knew that the rest of my life would be devoted to serving Jesus, my Master and my Savior.

Summary

The Old Testament foretold about Jesus' life and death, which saves all who believe in Him.

Teaching Tips

1. Read stories about Nicodemus in John 3:1–21; 7:45–52.

2. Read the story about the woman who met Jesus at a well and talked with Him alone in John 4:1–42. How is this story the same, and how is it different from the story of Nicodemus?

3. Why does Nicodemus want to see Jesus at night?

4. What does Nicodemus understand about Jesus' mission when he sees Him on the cross?

5. Work with your children to make a diorama of Jesus on the cross. Use your diorama to tell this story to someone, explaining why Jesus chose to die for us.

Midnight Request

Simon stepped carefully. The moon's absence made it more difficult to avoid crushing the flowers growing on his neighbor's property. Normally, he would not bother Silas this late at night, but he needed help. He carefully walked around to the back of the house where he knew Silas slept, then he whispered outside the window, "Silas! Silas! Wake up!"

There was no answer, so he tried again a little louder. "Silas! Silas! Are you awake?"

"Go away, Simon. It's cold, and it's late," Silas grumbled sleepily.

"Silas, I need your help," Simon insisted.

Annoyed, Silas rolled over and asked, "Why do you need my help at midnight? My house is locked up. My wife and children are asleep. And I *was* asleep until you woke me up. Go away! Return in the morning if you still need my help then."

"Please, Silas. Give me one minute to explain my situation."

This chapter is based on Luke 11:1–13 and Christ's Object Lessons, *chapter 12, "Asking to Give."*

Scripture

Ask and it will be given to you; seek and you will find; knock and the door will be opened to you.

—Luke 11:9

"Fine. Explain. I'll try to stay awake to listen." Silas rolled over in his bed with his back to the window.

"Oh, thank you, Silas. You see, my wife's brother and his family traveled the six miles from Capernaum to Bethsaida today. They wanted to surprise my wife and me and meet our new baby. They travel slowly with their children being so young. But in addition to that, their journey was delayed for hours when a regiment of Roman soldiers blocked the road. I'm not sure why the soldiers—"

Silas interrupted him. "You said one minute, Simon. Get to the point. What do you need?"

"Yes, yes. Sorry. Silas, we were not expecting visitors, and we are out of bread. They are very hungry from their journey. I know it's late, but could you give me three loaves of bread to help satisfy their hunger until morning when we can go to the market to buy more food?"

"You want me to leave my warm, comfortable bed to give you three loaves of bread?"

"It would be a great help to me and my family,

Silas." Simon pulled his cloak tighter around his shoulders to keep the cold away.

Simon overheard the muffled voice of Silas's wife: "Give him the bread so I can go back to sleep."

Frustrated even more now that his wife had awakened, Silas angrily muttered, "OK, OK! I'm getting the bread. Simon, meet me at the front door." He pulled back the covers on his bed.

"Blessings on you, my friend," said Simon when Silas handed him the loaves. "Maybe you would like to stop by and say hello to my brother-in-law. I think you met him at our wedding. Of course, that was many years ago. He's changed. I've changed. We've all changed and grown some gray hairs while caring for our families. Our children love being together."

Silas interrupted Simon once more. "Good night, Simon! I'm going back to bed."

"Yes, of course, Silas. Thank you for the bread!"

Simon hurried to return to his home as best as he could in the dark, happy that Silas had been willing to help him help others.

Summary

When we use the gifts God gives us to help others, we are doing what Jesus would do.

Teaching Tips

1. Read Luke 11:5–7, 11–13 to find out how Jesus compares God's willingness to give His followers the gift of the Holy Spirit with fathers giving gifts to their children. How are the two examples similar, and how do they differ?

2. Compare this story in Luke 11 with Philippians 4:19, where God promises to take care of all our needs. What do these verses help you understand about God?

3. Simon asks for bread to be able to share with others. What does this help you understand about prayer?

4. Ask your children who they would feel comfortable asking for help—no matter what time of day. Talk about what makes these people qualified to be on their lists. Then create a page with their contact information so your children will know how to reach out in an emergency.

5. Share with your children about a time when you had to make a "midnight request" from someone. How does your story, together with this parable and Luke 11:5–10, help you understand more about the kingdom of heaven?

Two Men Prayed

Matthew opened his eyes and then quickly squinted to give them time to adjust to the bright morning sun pouring through his window. *It's morning at last!* he thought. He rolled out of bed and pulled on simple clothes. Then he stumbled into the main room of his house where his wife, Hannah, was preparing their breakfast.

"Good morning, my sweet husband!"

"Morning," Matthew mumbled an answer.

"You look so tired. Did you sleep OK?" Hannah asked.

"Not much."

"Bad dreams?"

"Bad memories," said Matthew.

"Again?" Hannah asked.

"Yes, again. A noise or something woke me up, and I started thinking and—"

This chapter is based on Luke 18:9–14 and Christ's Object Lessons, *chapter 13, "Two Worshipers."*

Scripture

If you, L<small>ORD</small>, kept a record of sins, Lord, who could stand? But with you there is forgiveness, so that we can, with reverence, serve you.

—Psalm 130:3, 4

"And you couldn't fall back to sleep for hours," Hannah finished his sentence.

"That's right."

"Matthew, maybe you would find peace if you went to the temple to pray. Why don't you go this afternoon to the service where the lamb will be sacrificed? God will listen to your heart."

"I just don't feel like God would even want me to talk to Him."

"Why not?"

"Hannah, I'm a tax collector! I've cheated people and acted badly. I wouldn't know where to begin to correct my bad choices. I could never find all the people I have overcharged to ask for their forgiveness and offer restitution. And that is only one of my worries!"

"Matthew—"

"My mind races from one bad choice to another as I think about my life. How could God ever love me?"

"Matthew, remember the psalm: 'If you, LORD, kept a record of sins, Lord, who could stand? But with you there is forgiveness, so that we can, with reverence, serve you' [Psalm 130:3, 4]. Go to the temple and pray today. I'm sure God will hear your heart."

* * * * *

On the same day, in another house in a different part of town, a second man woke up with the sun.

"What a brilliant day it is! *Hmm.* What is on my schedule today? Oh yes! It's my day to go to the temple and pray," said Azariah. He put on his best clothes and marched out to the main room of his house where his wife, Milcah, was preparing their breakfast.

"Good morning, Azariah."

"Ah! Good morning, my beautiful wife."

"You are certainly in a good mood today," said Milcah.

"And why should I not be? I have strong children, a fancy house, and a good reputation in the community. People look up to me. They follow my example."

"Did you sleep well?"

"Of course! I fell asleep counting all the money I gave away this week. You know what the Bible says: 'The righteous give generously' " (Psalm 37:21).

"Will you go to the temple this afternoon to pray while the lamb is sacrificed?" Milcah asked.

"You remembered!" Azariah said.

"Actually, I didn't remember," confessed Milcah. "But you always wear your fanciest robe when you visit the temple, and you have it on today."

"One must never enter the house of God wearing anything less than the best. People are watching me. What would they think if I wore simple clothes? My influence with them might be less—much less."

"When you are at the temple, will you please pray for my brother? He has been ill for two months now, and a blessing from God would be so helpful."

"If I remember, I will pray for him. I have a great number of things already on my list to tell God," replied Azariah. "Is breakfast ready? Yesterday was my day of fasting. It's not much of an inconvenience to go without food for a day, but today I am very hungry!"

"Yes, it's ready," Milcah sighed. "I'm sure God will hear your heart when you pray."

* * * * *

Azariah and Matthew arrived at the temple within minutes of each other, though neither one noticed the other.

Azariah paraded up the steps as his long, luxurious robe flowed behind him. He looked to the right and then to the left, waving at those he recognized and stepping farther away from those he looked down on. When he reached the temple doors, he entered with a dramatic sweep after one of the other worshipers opened it for him. He looked around and found a highly visible space in the center of the room. He gladly filled the spot, even though the location was tainted by a tax collector kneeling within his sight.

Finally, after straightening his robe, boldly clearing his throat, pulling out his list, and looking around to make sure many people were watching him, Azariah lifted his head in prayer. He began, "God, I thank you that I am not like other people—robbers, evildoers, adulterers—or even like this tax collector." He paused with a loud sniff to look at Matthew before continuing. "I fast twice a week and give a tenth of all I get" (Luke 18:11, 12). He continued to pray down his long list.

At the end of the prayer, he looked around, satisfied that he had spoken loudly enough for God—and everyone else—to hear about his righteous deeds.

Matthew, on the other hand, had found a place over in the corner. He overheard the Pharisee in his fancy robe praying about his good deeds. It made

Summary

Jesus hears our hearts when we pray. He longs to forgive us and give us peace.

Matthew feel even less worthy to pray, but then he remembered the promise Hannah had shared from Psalms. With all his heart, he longed for the forgiveness and peace offered in those words.

Matthew bowed his head to the ground. His sins weighed heavily on his heart. Because of his sorrow and grief, he could only whisper, "God, more than anything, I long to be accepted by You. God, have mercy on me, a sinner" (see Luke 18:13).

Peace filled Matthew, and he knew God had heard his heart.

Two men walked home from the temple that day. One continued to make sure God—and his neighbors—noticed his righteousness. The second man noticed his neighbors and asked God, with a grateful heart, for wisdom and love to know how to best serve Him by serving them.

Teaching Tips

1. Compare this parable Jesus told about prayer with the story about the servant who asks his king for forgiveness (Matthew 18:21–35). What do these stories teach about forgiveness?

2. What does Matthew 11:29 mean when Jesus talks about "rest for your souls"?

3. Jesus said that the tax collector went home "justified before God" (Luke 18:14). Why?

4. Ask your children to draw a picture in their journals of what was in the heart of the Pharisee and what was in the heart of the tax collector.

5. Work with your children to write a short skit where you pretend to be a news reporter who is interviewing people leaving the temple. Interview the tax collector and the Pharisee. What would they say to a reporter? Make sure the reporter shares his or her thoughts on the interviews with the two worshipers. Share your skit.

Keep Asking

Hannah stood in line waiting for her turn to speak to the judge. Initially she hoped for a short wait and quick resolution, but as the line advanced slowly, she realized that her turn likely wouldn't come that day and she would have to endure a longer delay before receiving the justice she deserved.

A cruel accident had led to the death of her husband during the summer. She had no male relatives except her two young sons. Together they had done the hard work of caring for the field of wheat her husband had planted before he died. But the week before the harvest, her neighbor Ebed had let his cows graze in her field, leaving the grain trampled and worthless. And she desperately wondered, *How will I pay our bills?*

Hannah now waited to ask the judge for help with collecting payment for the grain from Ebed. However, as the sun reached the tips of the mountains on the horizon, the judge announced, "The rest of you return tomorrow. I'm going home." He stood up and started to walk away.

A grumble crawled through the men in the crowd and dripped down the street

Scripture

Do not be anxious about anything, but in every situation, by prayer and petition, with thanksgiving, present your requests to God. And the peace of God, which transcends all understanding, will guard your hearts and your minds in Christ Jesus.

—Philippians 4:6, 7

This chapter is based on Luke 18:1–8 and Christ's Object Lessons, *chapter 14, " 'Shall Not God Avenge His Own?' "*

as they left the courtyard. Hannah panicked. *Who will watch my boys tomorrow? I can't ask my friend to give up her day again.*

As the crowd cleared, Hannah moved closer to the judge. "Please, sir! Be kind enough to hear my case today," she boldly called to the judge. "My enemy will ruin me!"

The judge slowed his exit and turned his neck to find the source of the voice calling to him.

"What is your name?"

"I am Hannah, widow of Elah."

"I'm sure you have an interesting story, Hannah, widow of Elah, but I'm done listening to stories today. Return tomorrow." The judge ended the exchange by leaving Hannah standing alone in the courtyard.

Hannah's face twisted with frustration. She walked home as the sun slipped behind the mountains. *I will ask him for help again tomorrow,* she decided on the way home. *I'll bring my boys with me if I have to!*

The next morning she again stood in line, waiting for her turn to speak to the judge. The birds flitting from tree to tree in the cool of the morning had entertained her boys temporarily. But now the heat silenced the birds as they sat in the shade of leafy branches. She wished for some shade for herself as she held her shawl out to provide shade for her boys.

"We're hungry," her boys begged her at the same time the judge made his announcement.

"Time for lunch. You can all wait here or return this afternoon. I'll be gone for an hour or two."

A few men in the waiting crowd started to follow the judge. She recognized her neighbor Ebed as one of them. Was he a friend of the judge?

Once again Hannah panicked. Her boys could not sit through the heat of the day to wait for the judge to return. "Please, kind sir! Hear my case before you leave!" Hannah called out.

Again, the judge slowed his exit and turned to see who was talking. "Weren't you here yesterday?" he asked Hannah.

Hannah moved closer to the judge and knelt before him. "Yes, I am Hannah, widow of Elah."

"I remember you. Come back later." With that, the judge and his friends left the courtyard.

Hannah knew her boys could not wait out the afternoon. Besides, she had work to do at home to prepare their simple evening meal, and she needed to give her goats water. At least the goats could eat some of the trampled grain. She struggled to keep back her angry tears. As she walked home, she decided, *I* will *return tomorrow to ask for justice!*

In fact, Hannah returned day after day. The judge always had a reason to put off listening to her case.

Today I won't wait for the judge to be ready to leave to ask for justice, Hannah thought. *I'm tired of waiting for all the men to state their cases first.*

Hannah woke her boys before sunrise and packed a meager breakfast for them. They left their house in the dark and made their way to the courtyard, arriving before anyone else. Hannah sat her boys down in front of the judge's chair and let them lean against her legs when their sleepy eyes closed. After sunrise, others arrived to wait for the judge, and they were surprised to see Hannah.

When the judge finally came into the courtyard, he looked at Hannah and rolled his eyes.

Hannah did not wait to speak. "Please, sir! Be kind enough to hear my case. I am in great need of justice."

"OK, OK! State your case," the judge said. "I'm tired of seeing you here, and I don't want you to start attacking me with your cries for help when you see me in the streets."

At last, Hannah had a chance to tell her story. "I seek payment from my neighbor whose cattle ruined our field of wheat. Without it, my sons and I are struggling to buy food and pay our debts."

"Who is your neighbor?" asked the judge.

"His name is Ebed, sir."

"Ebed? I know him. Though I don't fear God, and I don't care what people think, I will give you justice. Ebed will pay you back five times what the grain would have sold for. Expect him to bring the money to you by the end of the week. And don't bother me anymore!"

"Thank you! Thank you, kind sir. You have restored my life and the lives of my sons."

Hannah gathered her boys and left the courtyard with a happy heart, grateful for the ruling of the judge and thankful that the God of heaven had heard her prayers for justice.

Summary

Jesus wants us to talk to Him. He will listen to our prayers.

Teaching Tips

1. Luke explains in Luke 18:1 that Jesus told this story to help His followers understand that they should not give up praying. Read Matthew 6:5–13, where Jesus tells His followers how to pray. What do these two Bible passages help you understand about prayer?

2. Why does the judge ignore the woman's requests?

3. Why does the judge finally decide to help the woman?

4. The story of the persistent widow illustrates that God wants to help us in our troubles. Share stories about a time when God helped you in a difficult situation.

5. Work with your children to make a poster that shares Jesus' instructions about prayer, and include the information learned in this parable and Matthew 6. Share the poster with someone who wants to learn about Jesus.

Seth, the Shepherd Boy

"Seth, you have helped Joab for several months, and now you are old enough and wise enough to take the sheep out by yourself tomorrow. While you watch the sheep, I need Joab to help me plant the fields. I know you will do a good job of caring for the sheep," Seth's abba told him as the family ate their supper together one evening.

Seth, the youngest son, knew that soon he would be caring for the sheep by himself. *I guess I'm growing up. Abba trusts me to do a good job,* he thought.

In the morning, as Seth dressed to take out the sheep, Joab said to him, "Here, Seth, you'll need my leather shepherd's girdle so that you can easily carry a lamb if one gets tired. Take my rod and my staff so you'll be prepared if a wild animal comes. And here's my sling. You'll do a good job."

Then Seth's ima brought him Joab's shepherd's bag where she had packed his lunch. She said, "Take the ram's horn. I filled it with oil in case one of the sheep gets a cut or a scratch. And, of course, you'll want the little reed flute to play music so you won't be lonely."

This chapter is based on Luke 15:1–10 and Christ's Object Lessons, *chapter 15, " 'This Man Receiveth Sinners.' "*

He was ready. He put the flute in the bag and placed its strap, along with the one for the ram's horn, over his shoulder. He carried the rod and the staff and went out to the sheepfold where his family's sheep were sheltered with those of the neighbor. His abba approached him, and Seth asked, "Abba, will the sheep know my voice and follow me?"

"I think they will, Seth. That's one of the reasons I had you go with Joab for several months. Now the sheep should recognize your voice too. Let's see what happens."

Seth opened the door of the sheepfold and called to the sheep. They heard his voice and came out of the sheepfold, following him as he led them to the pasture. *I see Rosie has a new lamb. I'll have to watch to see if it can keep up. It's a boy lamb. He needs a name. Let's call him Skippy.* Watching the frisky lambs play together made him smile.

When the sun was high in the sky, Seth knew he needed to lead the sheep to water. They had to walk a long way to a stream with a quiet pool where the sheep liked to drink.

Skippy seemed tired, so Seth picked him up and rewrapped the girdle to make a space to carry the tiny lamb. At the pool, Seth set Skippy down next to Rosie, who was drinking some water. Skippy joined her, drank some of her milk, and then with fresh energy, joined the other lambs as they played in the sunshine.

As they walked to another pasture, Seth saw Sparky, one of the older lambs, starting to wander away from the others. He used his sling to land a small pebble a little ahead of Sparky, who turned back to join the others. Seth was glad for all the times he and Joab had practiced with the sling.

Later in the afternoon, the sheep rested in the shade, and Seth got out his flute to play some melodies. Out of the corner of his eye, he saw a movement under a bush. He jumped up quickly and saw it was a wolf. He grabbed his sling, put a stone in it, swung the sling, and let the stone go. It hit the wolf, and the animal slunk away.

The setting sun told Seth it was time to take the sheep back to the fold. He called to the sheep as they started back home to the sheepfold. The sheep walked faster, as if they were glad to be going home. Seth counted the sheep, one by one, as they entered the fold. "Oh no, one sheep is missing! It's the older lamb, Sparky," Seth called out to his brother.

"This is what you must do. Do you know where you last saw the lamb? Retrace your steps, and you will find him," Joab told him.

"Yes, it was near the pasture where I chased away a wolf this afternoon," Seth remembered.

"Go quickly. That wolf would love to catch Sparky," Joab said.

Seth prayed as he hurried back to their afternoon pasture. *Please, God, help me find Sparky!*

Seth sang to keep up his courage. His singing might warn the wolf that a human was nearby and coming to rescue the lamb.

Soon he thought he heard a faint sound, so he paused his song and listened. *Yes*, he heard it again. "*Baa, baa.*"

It must be Sparky! he thought as he turned his steps to follow the sound. Again, he heard, "*Baa, baa*," and this time it was louder.

As he came to a big rock, Sparky's cry was clear. "*Baa, baa.*" And there, in a hole beside the rock, he found the lamb.

Seth lifted Sparky onto his shoulders and happily sang out, "Thank You, God. You helped me find Sparky. My family will be so happy to know he is safe."

Arriving home, Seth opened the door to the sheepfold, lifted Sparky from his shoulders, and set him inside with the other sheep.

Seth closed and locked the sheepfold door, and then he ran into the house, shouting, "I found him! I found Sparky! He is safe with the other sheep."

The family gathered around the table, shouting, "Hurrah! Praise God! The lost is found!"

Several weeks later, Seth had the chance to hear Jesus tell stories about the Good Shepherd caring for His sheep. *I understand what He means!* Seth thought.

And when he heard Jesus say, "I am the Good Shepherd. The Good Shepherd lays down His life for the sheep" (see John 10:11), Seth decided, *Jesus loves me. He would even die for me. I always want to be His sheep.*

Teaching Tips

1. Read and compare the lessons found in Luke 15:3–7 and John 10:1–18.

2. What does Jesus mean when He says, "I am the Good Shepherd"?

3. Why is Jesus' message so important to Seth?

4. Why doesn't the shepherd leave the lost sheep and not look for it when he has so many other sheep?

5. Think about someone who needs help. Talk with your family about how you could share the love of Jesus and help that person. Work with your children to complete your plan

Summary

Jesus looks for us if we wander away from Him.

Elizabeth's Tenth Coin

Scripture

But God demonstrates his own love for us in this: While we were still sinners, Christ died for us.

—Romans 5:8

Grinding grain is not *my favorite job*, Elizabeth thought. She examined the flour she had ground into the clay bowl on her table, and then she sighed in relief. *Good! I'm done for today. There is plenty of flour to make bread for our supper.*

She mixed the flour, yeast, salt, oil, and water to make the dough while she thought of her beloved Aaron. She giggled a bit because she knew that the moment he came into the house, he would say, "*Mmm.* It smells so good in our home! My wife, Elizabeth, makes the best bread, and I am the lucky man who gets to eat it." Then he would give her a big hug, sit down at the table, and listen while she told him all about her day. She loved sharing her stories with Aaron.

Elizabeth finished kneading the dough and set the bowl on a corner of the table to give the bread time to rise. She cleaned her hands and pushed her hair back from her forehead. Then she brushed the flour from the front of her dress—and that's when she panicked. She noticed that one of the coins on the chain around her neck was missing!

She quickly removed her chain and counted the coins from her dowry attached

This chapter is based on Luke 15:1–10 and Christ's Object Lessons, *chapter 15, " 'This Man Receiveth Sinners.' "*

to it. *One, two, three, . . . eight, nine. Only nine? There are supposed to be ten!* She wondered, *Did it drop into the dough? No, I would have felt it when I kneaded the dough. It's not there.*

Oh, it's so dark in this house! I need to light my lamp so I can see better. Too bad the windows are so small!

Elizabeth lit a lamp, picked up her broom, and promised herself, *I will sweep every inch of this floor until I find my missing coin.*

First, she swept under the table, stirring up a great deal of dust, but no coin.

Next, she swept under the bed mats. Here she found her warmest scarf but not the coin.

Then she moved the furniture to the center of the room and swept in all the corners. She found a sewing needle, a broken piece of a bowl, and more than one spiderweb but still no coin.

Elizabeth didn't give up. She looked around the room and realized she had not moved the three oil jugs behind the table. She carefully set them on the table and swept some more. She found a mostly spent candle and a dead moth. And then on the stone floor in a crack between the stones, she saw her coin!

"I found it! I found my lost coin!" she exclaimed happily. She ran out of her house and over to her neighbor's door.

"Lydia! I found my lost coin!"

"You lost a coin?" Lydia asked.

"Yes, I noticed it was missing right after I finished kneading the bread for our supper."

"Oh no! Did you find it?"

"Yes! I found it," exclaimed Elizabeth. "It was caught between two of the stones on the floor, near where I store the oil jugs."

"What a relief!" Lydia clapped her hands. "Who knows what Aaron would have done if he came home and found one of your coins was missing!"

"Let's go tell Anna," insisted Elizabeth.

Together the two women ran to Anna's house nearby. After they repeated Elizabeth's story, Anna ran outside and loudly announced, "Everybody! You have to hear Elizabeth's story! Take a break from your work and join us."

In a few minutes, the neighboring women had gathered around Elizabeth.

"I have found my lost coin!" Elizabeth said excitedly.

She was peppered with questions from her friends.

"What happened?"

"How did you lose it?"

"Where did you find it?"

"I lit a lamp, moved furniture around, swept everywhere, and there it was, in a crack on the floor. See! It goes right here on my chain." Elizabeth pointed to the spot. "I'm so relieved to find it!"

"Do you think Aaron would have been angry with you for losing one of your dowry coins?" Anna asked.

Elizabeth shuddered. "I don't think so. But it doesn't matter now!" She said, "Rejoice with me; I have found my lost coin" (Luke 15:9).

The neighbors formed a circle and danced while they sang a song of thanks. Their hearts were light and happy for their friend Elizabeth.

When the women returned to their own homes, Elizabeth went to finish making her bread. She formed the dough into two loaves and let them rise a second time while she sewed the coin back onto her chain. All the while, she thought, *What a joyful story I have to share with Aaron tonight!*

Teaching Tips

1. Read the original parable in Luke 15:8–10, and then compare it with the story Jesus tells about a lost sheep in Luke 15:3–9. What do these stories teach you about how God looks for people?

2. Who do the woman and the lost coin in this parable represent?

3. Why is the woman so concerned about her coin?

4. What does the fact that the coin can't find itself help you understand about the kingdom of heaven?

5. Hide some money in your house for your children to find. Tell your children you will not tell where it is or give any hints—no matter how frustrated they become while looking for it. Arrange an agreement that your children can keep the money if they find it within ten days. Then, have your children start looking for the money. Have your children pay attention to how they feel while they are looking for the money and how they feel when they actually find it. Can the money do anything to help your children find it? How does Romans 5:8 fit with this story?

Summary

Jesus celebrates when His lost followers are found.

Hunger Pangs

Scripture

*Who is a God like you,
who pardons sin. . . .
You will again have
compassion on us; you
will tread our sins
underfoot and hurl all
our iniquities into the
depths of the sea.*

—Micah 7:18, 19

As Micah started his long walk home, he thought about everything that happened since he left his village. First, he had asked Amram, his abba, for his share of the family money he would receive after his abba's death. And yes, everyone thought he wished that his father would go ahead and die. After listening to his request, his abba sold some land and animals, then gave Micah his share of the inheritance.

Taking his money, Micah went to a faraway town, made new friends, and enjoyed spending his money on whatever he wanted. One day Micah realized his money was gone, and all at once, his new friends didn't want to be friends with him anymore. As if that wasn't bad enough, the area Micah was living in experienced a famine. There he was, penniless, friendless, and very hungry. Desperate to survive, Micah ended up herding and feeding pigs—an unclean job and a disgrace for a Jewish person. But Micah was so hungry that he wished he could eat some of the pigs' food.

As Micah thought about his situation, he realized that going home and asking to be a servant in his father's house would be better than starving while caring

This chapter is based on Luke 15:11–32 and Christ's Object Lessons, *chapter 16, " 'Lost, and Is Found.' "*

for pigs. So he left the pigs and began the long walk home, thinking to himself, *My father may not speak to me, and I'm certain my older brother, Jonas, will be angry with me. The people in the village will hate me; maybe they'll even throw things at me!*

Micah prepared his speech step-by-step. *Abba, I have sinned against heaven and against you. Let me be one of your hired servants. I will work hard for you. Please, Abba, forgive me.*

However, the closer he got, the more he worried about how people would treat him—especially his abba and his brother. Would Abba pretend he didn't know him? Would his brother speak to him? At the edge of the town, he saw a group of boys and thought to himself, *I look so different dressed in rags. I hope they don't recognize me.*

But as Micah walked through the gate into the village, he saw something unusual. A man was running—running toward him. This was strange because grown men did not run. Micah wondered, *Why is this man running? Wait! He looks familiar. Who can he be?*

As the man drew closer, Micah knew who he was. *Abba! What will he do? What will he say?*

The man ran faster, closing the distance, and then he grabbed Micah in a big hug, "Micah! Micah! My son!" He kissed Micah on both cheeks and called out to one of his servants who had followed him, "Jacob, go get my best robe. Micah will wear it."

Then he turned as more of his servants arrived. "All of you, prepare a banquet to celebrate my son's return."

The crowd that witnessed this reunion stared with their mouths open. And they wondered and whispered to each other. "This is Micah, the son who asked for his father's money. What kind of man welcomes back such a bad son? If Micah were my son, I would beat him, but Amram welcomed him home. Amazing!"

"I'm inviting you all to a feast at my house tonight to rejoice over my lost son's return," Amram said to the crowd.

That evening, after the servants had prepared the feast, Micah wore his father's best robe. The community gathered to celebrate, even though they were shocked at how Amram treated Micah.

But Jonas, Micah's older brother, had been working in the field and missed all the excitement of his brother's return home. So when he came home, he was astonished to hear music and dancing, smell delicious food, and see the neighbors dressed for the feast.

"What is this?" he asked one of the servants.

"Micah has returned! Your father is so happy that he had us prepare this feast. Come in, and join the party," the servant explained.

"My brother? The one who demanded so much money? Why would Father have a party for him?" Jonas asked angrily.

Some of the guests heard his shouting and wondered what Amram would do. But Amram simply went outside and spoke quietly to Jonas. "Your brother, my son, was dead as far as we were concerned. Now he is home. I love him just like I love you. My son is found. Of course, I must express my joy."

"But he doesn't deserve anything! You never even let me have a party with my friends. Then this good-for-nothing boy comes home, and you celebrate with a huge feast. Abba, this is so unfair. I've served you faithfully! What have you given me?" Jonas demanded.

Some of the guests whispered together. "Look at Amram's sons. One took his inheritance and wasted it. The other is rude to his father and won't even greet the guests or play his role as host of the party. Amram is a good, kind man, but his sons are both disgraceful."

Teaching Tips

1. Read the stories that Jesus told about a lost sheep (Luke 15:4–7) and a lost coin (Luke 15:8–10). How are they the same, and how are they different from the story of the lost son?

2. What does Jesus want us to learn from these stories? What do they help you understand about God's kingdom?

3. Which son, Micah or Jonas, treated his father worse? Why do you think so?

4. Jesus leaves the story without an ending. Will Jonas show respect to his father and understand that as his father loves Micah, he also loves him? The people in Jesus' audience acted like the older brother. Will they learn that they need to accept repentant sinners as God does? Ask your children to write or draw an ending to the story in their journals and share them with you.

5. Share about a time when you knew God had forgiven you. Do your children have an experience to share with you?

Summary

Jesus offers total love to all, even those who turn their backs on Him.

Leaves Without Figs

Scripture

But the fruit of the Spirit is love, joy, peace, forbearance, kindness, goodness, faithfulness, gentleness and self-control.

—Galatians 5:22, 23

One day, Tabitha and her children, Jesse and Rachel, were at the temple.

"Look, there's Jesus." Jesse pointed to a large crowd. "Please, Ima, can we go listen to Him?" he asked.

"Yes, Ima, please, please. I want to hear Him!" Rachel added.

Ima nodded, and the family joined the crowd.

Just then, Jesus started telling a story. "A man and his gardener went together to inspect his orchard. The owner was happy with the many trees that had fruit or blossoms for more fruit. Suddenly, he said to his gardener, 'Look at this fig tree. Leaves, leaves, and more leaves but not a single fig. For the last three years, it's always been the same story. Gardener, you must cut it down so we can plant something else.'

" 'Sir, let's spare the tree another year. I will dig around it and fertilize it. Surely, it will bloom and have good figs,' the gardener pleaded.

" 'All right,' the master agreed, 'but if there is no fruit next year, it will be cut down.' "

This chapter is based on Luke 13:1–9 and Christ's Object Lessons, *chapter 17, " 'Spare It This Year Also.' "*

The family listened to more of Jesus' stories, but all too soon, Tabitha told her children, "We have to go home now. Your abba will come home soon, and he'll be hungry."

As they walked home, Rachel said, "I love listening to Jesus and His stories, but sometimes I don't know what they mean."

"Yes, Ima. What do you think the story about the fig tree meant?" Jesse asked.

"Jesus' stories have a deeper meaning, maybe even more than one. Maybe this story has some political meaning. I'm not sure. But it definitely has a spiritual meaning. Any ideas what it could be?" their mother asked.

"Do you think that the tree might mean us?" Jesse asked.

"You could be right," Tabitha answered. "What would be the meaning of the flowers and the figs?"

"I know, I know," Rachel said excitedly. "They could mean good things in our lives, such as kindness and patience."

"I'm proud of you, my daughter," Ima said. "Those are the good qualities Jesus wants us to have in our lives and in how we treat others. What other qualities would Jesus want us to have?"

"Faithfulness, goodness, peace, and love," Jesse replied. "But, Ima, how can I become kinder and more loving?"

"I know! When I listen to Jesus, I feel more loving," Rachel said.

"Remembering what I learn from the Scriptures helps me too," Ima said.

"Do you mean that trusting in Jesus and the words from the Scriptures changes me?" Jesse asked.

"Yes, you're right, my son," Ima agreed. "Do you remember how we made bread together last week?"

"It was fun," said Rachel.

"And it tasted so good," Jesse added.

"Oh, now I remember. Having Jesus in our hearts changes us like the leaven makes the bread dough rise," Rachel said.

"And having Jesus in our hearts makes His fruit of love, joy, peace, patience, kindness, goodness, faithfulness, gentleness and self-control grow in our lives," Ima explained.

As they arrived at their front door, Ima asked Jesse and Rachel to help her fix dinner for their abba.

"I'm glad that we were able to hear Jesus today. What a blessing for all of us! May these good fruits grow on your trees."

"We want to follow Jesus always and learn from Him so His fruits will grow in us," both children insisted.

Teaching Tips

1. Read this parable in Luke 13:6–9.
2. Why does the owner want to cut down the fig tree?
3. Why does the gardener want to let it grow another year?
4. How can you grow fruit for Jesus?
5. Work with your children to draw a cartoon strip to illustrate this parable and use it to explain the story to some younger children.

Summary

When we focus on Jesus, we allow the Holy Spirit to grow His fruits in our hearts.

An Invitation to the Fabulous Feast

Scripture

But because of his great love for us, God, who is rich in mercy, made us alive with Christ even when we were dead in transgressions—it is by grace you have been saved.

—Ephesians 2:4, 5

"Master, everything is ready," Hiram's servant reported. "The cooks have prepared the finest roasts, the prettiest platters of fruit, and delightful desserts. Your guests will be treated like royalty!"

"Excellent, Simon! Please let my friends know the feast is ready, and I am so looking forward to sharing this special meal with them," replied Hiram.

"Yes, Master. I am honored to be your messenger."

Simon decided to visit the home of Benjamin first. He was one of Hiram's most trusted friends.

Simon knocked on Benjamin's door. When it opened, he announced, "Master Benjamin! Master Hiram asked me to tell you that everything is ready for the feast he invited you to."

"What's that?" Benjamin asked.

"Master Hiram asked me to tell you that his feast is ready."

This chapter is based on Luke 14:1, 12–24 and Christ's Object Lessons, chapter 18, " 'Go Into the Highways and Hedges.' "

"Oh, that," Benjamin grumbled. "Um, er, I will not be able to make it to the feast, Simon."

"Excuse me, Master Benjamin. I am confused. You already promised you would attend."

"Well, that was last week. Since then, I've bought a piece of land, and I made an appointment to inspect it today. I'm sure Hiram will understand. Please let him know."

"You didn't inspect the land before you bought it?" Simon asked.

"That's really none of your business. No more questions."

"Yes, Master Benjamin," Simon replied slowly and turned away.

Simon stopped next at Ezra's house. Surely Master Hiram's closest business associate would be happy to hear the news. He stepped up to the door, knocked, and called into the open window. "Master Ezra! Master Hiram asked me to tell you that everything is ready for the feast he invited you to attend."

Simon heard no answer, so he called again, "Master Ezra?" And then he heard a crash in the barn. *Ah, Master Ezra is in the barn.*

He walked over to the open door and called,

"Master Ezra! Master Hiram asked me to tell you that everything is ready for his feast."

"Just a minute!" Ezra responded.

Simon heard a few more bangs and clunks, then watched Ezra exit the barn, dressed in his work clothes.

"Did you say Hiram's feast is ready?"

"Yes, Master Ezra. He sent me to call you for the meal."

"Too bad. I'm busy today. I'm on my way to see the ten oxen I recently purchased. I need to see whether the animals work well together. You'll have to let Hiram know I won't make it to his feast."

"Forgive me for asking, Master Ezra. Did you buy the oxen without testing them first?"

"As a matter of fact, I did. The price was a bargain. I knew testing them today would conflict with Hiram's meal, but I'm sure he'll understand, just this once. Goodbye."

Simon hung his head and left.

Simon saw Master Ira in his front yard, dressed in a fancy robe, while he was still four houses away. *At last,* thought Simon, *one of Master Hiram's friends is ready for the feast!*

"Simon! Good to see you! How is my friend Hiram doing today?" Ira enthusiastically called out when Simon walked closer to the house.

"He is well, Master Ira! Master Hiram asked me to tell you that everything is ready for the feast he invited you to attend."

Ira's smile faded. "Oh, that's not good."

Simon looked at Ira with a puzzled expression.

Before he could ask for details, Ira added, "You may or may not remember that I am newly married as of a few weeks ago. I can't leave my bride to join him at his feast. Tell him I won't be there."

Simon didn't offer any arguments. He simply watched as Ira happily disappeared into his house.

Simon's heart was heavy for his master. Hiram had worked so hard to provide the very best feast possible, but his friends returned the gift with empty excuses.

Hiram paced the street in front of his house, waiting for Simon's return. When he saw Simon, he walked out to meet him.

"Are they on their way?" Hiram inquired.

"Well, Master Hiram, actually, none of them will be joining you for the feast." Then Simon shared Benjamin's, Ezra's, and Ira's excuses. "Master, their excuses are empty. By not attending, they are publicly insulting you!"

"What you say is true," Hiram answered slowly and deliberately. "My friends make me feel angry because they are choosing to end their friendship with me." Hiram thought for a moment and then continued, "I have another job for you, Simon."

"Whatever you ask, I will do for you, Master."

"My feast is ready, but none of my friends chose to attend. So go out into the streets of the town and invite everyone—I want my table to be full!"

"Yes, sir! On my way!"

Hurriedly, Simon announced to everyone he saw, "Listen to this good news! Master Hiram asks you to join him now to share a special meal. Everything is ready and waiting."

Then he led the way to his master's house. He smiled as he saw the seats at the banquet tables filling up.

"Master," he said, "many people are sitting at your tables, but there is still room for more. Many of the people I invited have never talked to you before and may not feel worthy of your gift, Master."

Summary

We don't have to be worried about being good enough to be a part of Jesus' kingdom. His forgiveness is a gift.

"Go out again, Simon. Tell them I want to be their friend. That's why I'm inviting them," Hiram insisted.

Simon acted on his master's request, and soon the tables at the feast were filled to overflowing with grateful guests.

Teaching Tips

1. Jesus told this story to listeners at a Sabbath dinner to which He had been invited. Find it in Luke 14:15–24, and then read what He said to them right before He told this story (Luke 14:8–14). What do these verses teach about how Jesus feels about people?

2. What do the actions of the master in the story of the great banquet help you understand about Jesus and the kingdom of heaven?

3. Discuss what it means to accept and to decline the invitation to be Jesus' friend.

4. The next time you think about having a birthday party, brainstorm with your family and make plans to invite more than just your close friends. After the party, discuss how you were blessed by the presence (not *presents*) of your guests.

5. Tell your children about a time when you felt unworthy of forgiveness and a place in heaven. Ask your children to explain what they understand the words *grace* and *mercy* to mean and why. Then ask your children whether they ever worry about being "good enough" for heaven. Work with your children to start a collection of Bible promises about the assurance of forgiveness and salvation, and have your children write or draw them in their journals.

Debtor Forgiven

"Manasseh, the king wants to see you," called Ethan, the king's steward. "Right this way."

"I'm coming," Manasseh answered. The king was always pleased with his work in the treasury, so Manasseh was glad to be invited to talk to the king.

Entering the throne room, Manasseh bowed before the king and gave the usual greeting: "Oh, King, live forever. How may I serve you today?"

"Manasseh," the king said, "I have been checking all my accounts. I was surprised to learn how much you owe me. Ten thousand talents! That's an enormous sum! What has happened? Why have you not returned the money that I lent you?"

Manasseh quickly recalled the many times he had borrowed money from the king. First, it was feasts for his children's weddings. Then his wife wanted a new house. Lately, his son needed money to start his own business. Alas, the business failed.

"Your Majesty, I did borrow money for some family needs. And the business my son started did not do well. I am so sorry, but I have no money to pay you back."

"Well, Manasseh, if you have no money, you leave me no choice. I will have to

This chapter is based on Matthew 18:21–35 and Christ's Object Lessons, *chapter 19, "The Measure of Forgiveness."*

Scripture

Be kind and compassionate to one another, forgiving each other, just as in Christ God forgave you.

—Ephesians 4:32

put you in prison. Your property will be sold. Your wife and children will be sold into slavery. That is the law." The king's voice became angry. "How could you have wasted my money so outrageously?"

"Please, please, give me more time. I have always been faithful to you," Manasseh pleaded and dropped to his knees. "I will pay you back. Please have mercy!"

Manasseh's voice caught, knowing that the king could put him in debtor's prison, sell his house, and even sell his children into slavery. Swallowing hard, Manasseh thought, *How foolish I have been!*

"Manasseh, you have been faithful in all your work for me. Yes, I will give you more time. Wait, I will do something else. I will forgive your debt. You are free to go. Just continue your good work for me," the king said graciously.

Manasseh was speechless. He knew he didn't deserve mercy. Finally, he said, "Yes, Your Majesty. How can I thank you enough? Your generosity and kindness are amazing. I am your humble servant. Oh, King, may I go home to tell my wife? She will be so pleased."

"Yes, Manasseh, go home," he said.

"Thank you! Thank you," Manasseh called over his shoulder.

But as he left the palace, Manasseh saw Jesse, the king's stable boy, and thought, *Oh, good, I've needed to speak with Jesse. He owes me a hundred denarii.*

"Jesse, Jesse, I need to talk to you," Manasseh called out.

Jesse turned and said, "How are you, Manasseh? How can I help you?"

"Jesse, have you forgotten that you owe me money?" Manasseh asked.

"Yes, Manasseh, I owe you a hundred denarii. Please give me more time, and I will pay you."

"No, I need the money now. If you cannot pay me right this minute, you will have to go to debtor's prison."

"Manasseh, please have mercy. I will pay you," Jesse begged.

"Guard," Manasseh called, "please come get this man. He owes me money and cannot—or will not—pay me."

The guard came and tied Jesse's hands behind his back with rope as Jesse continued to beg. "Give me more time. I will pay you."

The noise attracted a number of the king's servants, and they saw Jesse being led away to prison.

Ethan recognized Jesse and Manasseh and asked, "Manasseh, why can't you give Jesse mercy when the king just forgave you so much more?"

Suddenly, several of the servants grabbed Manasseh by the arms and dragged him into the throne room. "Your Majesty, here is Manasseh, whom you just forgave ten thousand talents. Two minutes ago, he had Jesse, the stable boy, arrested and taken to jail for not repaying a debt of one hundred denarii."

Realizing anew how foolishly he had acted, Manasseh became terrified as the king looked at him sternly.

Finally, the king spoke, "You wicked servant. Why couldn't you give the stable boy mercy like I gave to you? Guards, take him away. Sell his property, including that house bought with my money. His wife and children shall be slaves. No more will they wear fancy clothes paid for with money Manasseh borrowed from me. Manasseh himself will be in prison at hard labor until he returns everything he has borrowed from me."

Summary

Because God has forgiven me, I can forgive others.

Teaching Tips

1. Read this story in Matthew 18:23–35.

2. Compare this parable with what Jesus teaches about forgiving others in the Lord's Prayer in Matthew 6:12, 14, 15.

3. What question about forgiving others did Peter ask just before Jesus told this story? What was Jesus' answer? See Matthew 18:21, 22.

4. Did Jesus mean that we should count how many times we forgive someone? Why do you think so?

5. Ask your children to write or draw in their journals about a time when someone forgave them, including how they felt. Share your own story too.

Balak Built a Bigger Barn

Scripture

And my God will meet all your needs according to the riches of his glory in Christ Jesus.

—Philippians 4:19

"Where's my breakfast? It's late!" roared Balak.

Immediately, Aaron came running from the kitchen. "Please forgive me, Master. The chickens escaped their coop early this morning, and I had to search for the eggs."

"Don't let it happen again," Balak growled. "I'm a busy man, and I need my breakfast on time. There's so much to do to manage my property, and soon it will be time for the wheat harvest. I have so much to do! Do you hear me?"

"Yes, Master. You have so much to do that breakfast can't be late."

"That's right! Now, put the food on the table so I can eat quickly and get to business!"

Aaron placed the tray of food in the spot preferred by his master, then silently left the room to attend to kitchen details. Soon he heard his name called.

"Aaron! Aaron! Where are you?" Balak barked.

This chapter is based on Luke 12:13–21 and Christ's Object Lessons, *chapter 20, "Gain That Is Loss."*

"Right here, Master."

"I've finished eating. Take the tray, and clean up the table. I need the space to spread out the plans for my new barn."

"A new barn, Master?"

"Yes, a new barn. My old one is much too small to hold what I'm expecting from the harvest."

Aaron hesitated before asking a question. "Master, are you sure a new barn is the best idea?"

"Of course, I'm sure! Why? Do you have a better idea?" Balak snapped.

"Well, I thought sharing the extra food with hungry people in town might be appreciated," Aaron suggested.

"Why did I even ask for your opinion? You're like all the other people who used to visit me. They pretended to have good intentions, but all they wanted was for me to give away my wealth. I won't! I've worked hard to be comfortable, and this harvest is no exception."

"You seem very comfortable, Master. There are others not nearly as fortunate as yourself," Aaron dared to mention.

"Get out! Take the dishes with you. And stop telling me what to do! I've already made my decision."

Aaron gathered the dishes and hurried to the kitchen.

* * * * *

In time, the bigger barn was built and filled with the wheat harvest by the temporary workers Balak found at the marketplace. Sure enough, the harvest yielded five times the amount gathered the previous year.

"I've worked so hard growing the wheat, and my hard work ensures I'll have plenty to eat for many years," Balak bragged to himself because no one ever stayed around to listen to him.

"It's time for some relaxation," Balak said as he strolled to his house after inspecting his new barn.

"Aaron! Aaron! Where are you?" Balak bellowed.

"Sorry, Master. The fire was about to go out, so I had to add more wood before I could greet you."

"Forget the fire. Bring me some wine. I will sit on the front porch and savor the view of the fine barn I designed."

"Yes, Master. I'll be back in a few minutes."

"Make it quick! I don't want to waste time that I

could spend enjoying myself."

Balak eased into his favorite chair and gazed at the barn with a wide smile. He thought about how high the hills of grain reached inside. Yes, his hard work had paid off, and he hadn't let anyone talk him out of keeping it all. *Good choice*, he congratulated himself.

Balak rubbed his left shoulder while he waited for Aaron. *I wonder why my arm hurts*. Then, without warning, he felt as if a large ox stood on his chest. His hands grabbed at the pain.

When Aaron returned with the wine, he found Balak slumped over in his chair as if he had fallen asleep.

"Here is your wine, Master," he said, but Balak did not move.

Aaron gently tapped Balak's arm. "Master," he repeated, "I've brought your wine."

Still Balak sat motionless.

Aaron placed the wineglass on the ground and anxiously shook Balak's shoulders. "Master? Master!" It was then that he realized Balak was not breathing. He felt for a heartbeat and found none.

Balak had no children, so his house, his barn, his harvest, and all his property were given to his brother, who gladly shared the abundance with those in need.

Teaching Tips

Summary

Jesus provides for our needs and asks us to share with those in need.

1. In the verses following the story of the rich fool (Luke 12:13–21), Jesus explains how to set our priorities. Read Luke 12:22–34. How do the decisions of the rich fool differ from the advice Jesus gives in Luke 12:22–34 and Matthew 6:19–21, where He talks about storing our treasure in heaven?

2. Why is building a bigger barn so important to Balak?

3. Why is it a problem that Balak identifies himself as the supplier of everything he needs?

4. Help your children find the words *greedy*, *selfish*, and *covetous* in a dictionary, and write down the meanings of the words in their journals. Write a term that means the opposite next to each word. Ask your children to write or draw a picture in their journals that explains the meaning of Luke 12:15, where Jesus talks about owning things.

5. As a gift of gratitude to God for His blessings, work with your children to develop a plan that creates opportunities to share their time, talents, or treasures with someone in need. Help make the plans happen.

Switching Places

Jesus replied: " 'Love the Lord your God with all your heart and with all your soul and with all your mind.' . . . And the second is like it: 'Love your neighbor as yourself.' "

—Matthew 22:37, 39

Once upon a time in a far-off land, King Michael ruled his subjects with loving-kindness and compassion. His kingdom had only two laws:

- Love the king with all your heart, mind, and soul.

- Love your neighbor as yourself. (Sometimes this law was described as treating others like you would want to be treated.)

In that far-off land lived a man named Nabal, who was very rich. King Michael had given him great wealth so he could help others. Nabal was so rich that he lived in a fancy house with lots of servants. Nabal often asked his servants to prepare a banquet for him and his invited guests.

In the same land, there lived a poor man named Lazarus. He was very sick, and he had no money to buy food or the medicine he needed to get well. Lazarus's friends carried him to Nabal's house every day, where he would lie on the ground near Nabal's gate in the hope that Nabal would notice him and help him. However, Nabal was always very busy attending his banquets with his friends. He had no time for Lazarus.

This chapter is based on Luke 16:19–31 and Christ's Object Lessons, *chapter 21, " 'A Great Gulf Fixed.' "*

Often Lazarus hoped he would be given the leftovers from some of the banquets. Unfortunately for Lazarus, the leftovers were always fed to Nabal's dogs.

Even the dogs noticed Lazarus, but day after day, Lazarus suffered while Nabal celebrated his rich life.

King Michael heard about Nabal and Lazarus and sent his soldiers to confirm the facts. When he found out the story was true, he told the soldiers to end Nabal's life of selfishness and luxury by arresting him and putting him in prison. He also instructed them to bring Lazarus to live in his palace, where he could enjoy banquets with the king and his prime minister, Abraham.

Naturally, Nabal was quite upset about his change in circumstances, so he sent a message to the prime minister. "It's not nice being in prison. Please send Lazarus to bring me something to make me more comfortable."

Abraham replied, "You lived in luxury while Lazarus lay on the ground outside of the gates of your property. Because you loved money more than King Michael, you became blind to the needs of others. Now Lazarus is comfortable here. He's not—nor has he ever been—your servant, and he can't visit you in prison."

Nabal sent Abraham a second message. "Then, please send Lazarus to my five brothers. They live lives of selfishness and luxury, just like I did. They need to be warned that they should change, so they won't end up in prison like me."

Abraham answered Nabal's second message. "Your brothers have the laws of King Michael. They should follow them."

Again, Nabal sent a message to Abraham. "No, that won't be enough to convince my brothers. But if they receive a special message from King Michael, then they would change."

However, Abraham responded, "The choices of your life prove the opposite, Nabal. Just like you, if your brothers don't listen to the laws of the king, then a special messenger won't change their minds either."

Summary

Jesus asks us to love Him more than we love anyone or anything else.

Teaching Tips

1. Find this story in Luke 16:19–31. Compare the lesson of this story with 1 Timothy 6:10, which talks about the problems of loving money.

2. Describe how you think Nabal feels about Lazarus before and after he is in prison.

3. What is Jesus trying to teach when He says that Nabal's dogs were kind to Lazarus?

4. Is it wrong for Nabal to prepare banquets for his friends? Why, or why not?

5. Help your children research the stories of three wealthy people who are philanthropists. Discuss how the members of your family can become philanthropists.

A Father's Request

Asher surveyed his family's vineyard. New branches had started growing, and it was time to thin the leaves and tie the new growth in place. He decided to ask his sons to help him complete the work.

Asher found Titus taking a nap in the shade of the fig tree in the front yard.

"Hey, Titus. Wake up! It's the middle of the morning." Asher nudged his son until his eyes opened.

"*Hmm*? Oh, hi, Abba," said Titus as he rubbed his eyes to wake up. "I sat down here to take a little rest after my morning walk, and I fell asleep. Did you want to ask me something?"

"The vineyard needs some attention. Can you help me this afternoon with managing the new growth so we'll have a good harvest this year?"

"What time?" asked Titus.

"If you meet me there after you finish your lunch, we should be able to complete the task in a few hours if we work together," explained Asher.

This chapter is based on Matthew 21:23–32 and Christ's Object Lessons, *chapter 22, "Saying and Doing."*

Scripture

I desire to do your will, my God; your law is within my heart.

—Psalm 40:8

"Sorry, Abba, I have plans this afternoon, and I won't have time for vine management."

"Plans? What kind of plans?" Asher asked.

"I have important business in town that must be handled today. But maybe I can help you tomorrow." With that, Titus closed his eyes and continued his nap under the fig tree.

The expression on Asher's face told of his disappointment as he walked away.

Next, Asher found Mark in the barn, cleaning out the animal stalls and organizing the farm tools. "Hi, Mark. The vineyard needs some attention. Can you help me this afternoon with managing the new growth so we'll have a good harvest this year?"

"Sure, Abba, I can help you. What time?" Mark asked.

"Meet me there after lunch. If we work together, we should be able to finish in a few hours."

"OK. I'll plan on it," Mark replied.

After lunch, Asher picked up his tools and walked to the vineyard. When he arrived, Mark wasn't there. *Something must have delayed him*, he thought.

Asher opened the gate and picked the southwest corner of the vineyard to start his task of trimming and thinning the leaves and new shoots. Some of the shoots, or new branches, he tied so they would stay in place. He also removed clusters of newly forming grapes where too many grew next to each other.

He had finished half of the first row when he heard the vineyard gate open. "Hi, Mark," he called without looking up.

"It's me, Abba, not Mark," responded Titus.

Asher turned, surprised to find Titus at the gate. "I'm happy to see you! But I thought you had important business to take care of in town this afternoon."

"Well, I decided helping you in the vineyard was more important," Titus answered. "How can I help?"

"If you tie up the vines on one side of this row and I do the same on the other, we'll be finished in half the time!"

"OK! I'm ready to work."

"Have you seen Mark?" Asher asked.

"Sure did. I saw him out on the road in front of the barn on my way over. His friend was showing off a new donkey colt," reported Titus. "It looked like they would be busy for quite a while."

"Thanks for your help, son. I'm grateful." Asher smiled. "Maybe Mark will join us before the afternoon is over."

Summary

Our actions show the focus of our hearts.

Teaching Tips

1. Find this parable in Matthew 21:28–32. Compare this parable with the story of Matthew being called to be a disciple of Jesus in Matthew 9:9–13. In both stories, there is a message to religious leaders. What are the messages? How are they the same, and how are they different?

2. Why does the father in this story ask both of his sons to help him in the vineyard?

3. The actions of both boys were the opposite of the answers they gave their father. Why?

4. Do you think Mark ever decides to help in the vineyard? Why, or why not?

5. Ask your children if there has been a time when they were asked to do something, and they told the person asking that they couldn't help. Did your children change their minds like Titus in this story? Why, or why not? Ask your children to write or draw the story in their journals.

Elam's Rented Vineyard

Scripture

May God be gracious to us and bless us and make his face shine on us—so that your ways may be known on earth, your salvation among all nations.

—Psalm 67:1, 2

"Abba, you've been away from the beautiful vineyard you planted for more than a year. I believe it's time to send a servant to see how the grapes are doing," advised Jonathan.

"Indeed, it's time. I think I'll send Elijah to bring back the portion of the fruit that belongs to me. Would you agree?" Jonathan's father, Elam, asked.

"Elijah is known as your faithful servant. Yes, send him."

Elam called for Elijah and explained, "Please go to my vineyard and talk with the renters. Bring back some of the fruit for us."

Elijah promised to return quickly, and he left on his mission right away. He was sure the meeting with the tenants would go well. Elam was a fair man.

However, several days later, Elijah stood before Elam and Jonathan with a bruised face and torn clothes. He limped into the room with the help of a crutch.

"What happened to you?" Elam asked.

This chapter is based on Matthew 21:33–44 and Christ's Object Lessons, *chapter 23, "The Lord's Vineyard."*

"I visited your vineyard, just like you requested, Master. I explained why you had sent me and spoke with the renters about the harvest. However, when I asked them for your portion of the fruit, they were unkind and refused to honor you as the owner of the vineyard. They forced me to leave empty-handed."

"I am so sorry, Elijah. You are my faithful servant, and you should not have been treated like this," responded Elam. "Go home and rest until your leg and your bruises have healed."

Elijah bowed respectfully, then limped out of the room.

"Abba, you could try sending Jeremiah. The renters might listen to him," suggested Jonathan after hearing Elijah's story.

So Elam explained the reason for the journey to Jeremiah. "I'm anxious to hear the news from my vineyard."

Jeremiah left the next morning to check on his master's property. The tree-covered hills on the horizon signaled that he was close, and he was glad to see the renters caring for the vineyard when he turned the next corner. He felt sure the renters would listen to him. Elam was a kind landowner.

Jeremiah approached the renters and cheerfully explained, "Master Elam sent me to ask about the harvest and collect his portion of the fruit."

"You want to know about the harvest? Well, it's none of your business. Get out of here, and stop bothering us!" they replied.

"But I am delivering Master Elam's message."

"We don't want to hear it," they insisted.

"But he is the owner of this vineyard," Jeremiah objected.

"Do you hear this man who keeps talking when we've told him to be quiet?" one renter asked the other.

"Sure do. How about we throw him into that dry cistern for a while? He can talk and talk and talk all he wants in there, and we won't have to listen," said the other.

The renters grabbed Jeremiah, beat him, and threw him into the empty water-storage tank. They left him there for several days before they pulled him out and forced him to leave the vineyard.

"Tell Master Elam that we don't owe him anything," the renters sneered.

When Jeremiah told Elam and Jonathan about the shameful treatment he received from the vineyard's renters, they were shocked.

"Maybe Hosea would be able to talk with the renters," proposed Elam.

So Elam asked Hosea to meet with him to discuss the task. Hosea obediently journeyed to Elam's vineyard. Unfortunately, the tenants treated him no better than Elijah or Jeremiah. They refused to hear the message from Elam. They beat Hosea and chased him away without giving him any of the fruit from the harvest.

"Father, I think I need to visit with the renters," urged Jonathan.

"Maybe you are right," sighed Elam. "You are my son, and I love you. For that reason, they will respect you as my representative. Maybe they will be ashamed of how they have treated my other servants and will finally listen to you."

Jonathan was hopeful as he approached his father's property. *The renters should be happy to see me*, he thought. *My father has treated them generously. He only asks for what is rightfully his part of the harvest.*

However, the renters saw Jonathan on the road before he arrived and created an evil plan. "Would you look at this! Elam has sent his son, Jonathan, to talk with us. How convenient! All we have to do is make sure the heir of the vineyard *never* returns home, and we will become its new owners."

When Jonathan did not return home, Elam grew worried and investigated. He soon discovered the unspeakable way the renters had treated his son.

He mourned deeply and made sure the evil tenants received punishment. He rented out his vineyard again, but this time to tenants who treated him and his servants with love and respect.

Teaching Tips

1. Read this story in Luke 20:9–18 and Matthew 21:33–44. How are the stories the same, and how are they different?

2. Elam and Jonathan are the father and son in this story. Who do they represent?

3. What do the vineyard and the renters represent?

4. Why was the meaning of this parable important to the people in Jesus' time? Why is it important to Christians today?

5. The renters of the vineyard didn't thank or respect Elam, his servants, or his son for the use of the vineyard. Purchase some grapes at a grocery store. While eating the grapes with your children, discuss ways to thank Jesus for being the Savior of the world.

Summary

Jesus looks at our lives for evidence that we have allowed the Holy Spirit to grow His fruits in our hearts. He loves to hear our praise when we thank Him for His plan to rescue us from sin.

The Wedding Banquet

Scripture

I delight greatly in the LORD; my soul rejoices in my God. For he has clothed me with garments of salvation and arrayed me in a robe of his righteousness.

—Isaiah 61:10

"They have refused the invitation to your son's wedding banquet, Your Majesty."

"I must not have heard you correctly, Caleb. Could you repeat what you just said?" King Joel asked.

"Yes, sir. The people you invited to your son's wedding banquet have refused to attend."

"Maybe they misunderstood the invitation. Please send three additional royal messengers to their city to let them know—*again*—that everything is ready for my son's wedding banquet. Say to them, 'The king invites you to join the celebration.' "

Caleb made the arrangements for the messengers to leave at once. King Joel anxiously waited for them to return.

When they didn't return quickly, King Joel said to Caleb, "Find out what has happened. The messengers should have been back days ago."

This chapter is based on Matthew 22:1–14 and Christ's Object Lessons, *chapter 24, "Without a Wedding Garment."*

After Caleb received reports from the king's soldiers, he told King Joel, "Your Majesty, the news is not good. According to witnesses in the city, your invitation was ignored by some of the people. Others did not treat your messengers well. It upsets me greatly to tell you that your faithful servants will not be able to return home right away."

"How could they do this to my son, my servants, and me?" King Joel was very angry. "Caleb, tell the commanders of my army to go and take care of that city!"

"Yes, sir," replied Caleb.

"One more thing," said King Joel. "My son's wedding banquet is ready, and none of the people I originally invited deserve to attend. However, I still want people to be there."

"You could send out messengers to invite other people," suggested Caleb.

"Yes, do that! Have the messengers invite everyone!" King Joel instructed joyfully. "And those wedding clothes that I had made for my guests? They were very costly, but they should be given freely to whoever accepts my invitation. I want them to be ready for the wedding celebration." The king was excited about filling the seats in his banquet hall.

Caleb got to work at once. He told the messengers, "King Joel wants you to stand on the street corners. Everyone you see should be invited to his son's wedding. Give wedding clothes to everyone who accepts the invitation as a gift from the king."

The servants did as they were told, and soon the king's table was filled with guests happily talking about King Joel's amazing invitation.

King Joel entered the banquet hall with a huge smile on his face. At last, the celebration could begin! He took a minute to look around at all the guests. Unfortunately, in the center of the room sat a man who made the king's smile fade.

King Joel walked over to the man. "Friend, where are the wedding clothes you were given to wear? How did you get into my son's wedding banquet without them?"

The man had no answer for King Joel.

The king called Caleb and sadly told him, "Have my soldiers escort this man outside."

"Yes, Your Majesty. Right away."

Summary

Followers of Jesus don't need to be afraid of being judged by God because the perfect life of Jesus covers all sin.

Teaching Tips

1. Read the original version of this parable in Matthew 22:1–14, and compare it with Isaiah 61:10. What do these verses help you understand about being a part of God's kingdom?

2. What does the wedding banquet represent?

3. Who do the king and his son represent?

4. Who does the man without wedding clothes represent?

5. Purchase a roll of red cellophane. On clean sheets of paper, have your children draw pictures with green markers. Then scribble over the drawings with a red marker. Cut out pieces of the red cellophane, and place them over the drawings. Note that the red scribbles disappear when the picture is viewed through the red cellophane. Ask your children to explain how this could be like Jesus' death on the cross takes care of our sins.

Invested

After Judah was asked to travel to a faraway country, where he would be named the ruler of the region, his servants busily packed his belongings for the journey.

When asked about his trip, Judah would say, "I don't know exactly how long I will be gone, but I *will* return."

A week before his trip, he invited ten of his trusted servants to a meeting.

Judah told them, "I asked you to visit with me because I want to give each of you some money. I would like you to invest it in businesses in my name. I look forward to hearing about your experience when I return."

Soon Judah's house settled into a quiet, peaceful routine with the master gone. However, the city gate, where the leaders gathered, was far from quiet and peaceful.

"I'm so glad Judah is gone," remarked one man. "I hope he never returns!"

"I hate him!" said another.

This chapter is based on Matthew 25:13–30 and Christ's Object Lessons, *chapter 25, "Talents."*

Scripture

Whatever you do, work at it with all your heart, as working for the Lord, not for human masters, since you know that you will receive an inheritance from the Lord as a reward. It is the Lord Christ you are serving.

—Colossians 3:23, 24

"I say we send a delegation to tell him we don't want him to come back," grumbled a third.

Some of the city leaders asked the servants at Judah's house, "How can you stand working for that—that man?"

One evening Anna, Reuben, and Thad sat together in the courtyard after the day's work was completed.

"I've decided to use the money to grow flowers to sell," Anna announced. "I'll sell them as Master Judah's Bouquets."

"I like your idea!" said her brother, Reuben. "I've decided to buy a small herd of milking goats. I'll sell Judah's Best Goat Milk at the market."

"What are your plans, Thad?" Reuben asked.

"Have you heard what the town leaders are saying about Master Judah?" Thad asked.

"I've heard," replied Reuben. "It doesn't matter to me. I believe Master Judah will return as the ruler of this region."

"But what if he doesn't return?" Thad insisted.

"He *will* return, Thad," Anna said without hesitation. "What are your plans for the money he gave you?"

"I'm still thinking. Some people hate Master Judah. I'm thinking about how things will go for my business if people know I work for him," answered Thad.

"Do you hate him?" Reuben asked.

"Of course not!" Thad said defensively.

"Then what does it matter what other people say?" Anna replied.

Anna and Reuben tended their projects. Anna's buttercups, marigolds, anemones, lilies, and other colorful blooms thrived under her care. The goats Reuben bought yielded a great quantity of milk because he provided for all their needs and comforts.

"I'll join you at the market tomorrow," announced Anna. "Can I set up my flower stand next to yours at the market?" she asked her brother.

"Of course, I would be delighted!" Reuben replied.

The next morning they loaded a cart and walked together to the market. On the way, they talked about Thad.

"I wish Thad were with us this morning," lamented Anna.

"Me too. I asked him again about his project last

week, and he just glared at me and said, 'I'm still thinking!' "

Over the next two years, Anna and Reuben invested large amounts of time in their master's businesses. Sometimes they talked about Master Judah's return and wondered when it would happen.

One day, when they returned from the market, they were overjoyed to see Master Judah's horse tied to one of the posts in front of the house.

"Master Judah has returned, just like he promised!" rejoiced Anna.

They could hardly wait to meet with him that same evening.

"I am happy to share the news that I have been appointed as your king," explained Judah.

"Long live King Judah!" cheered the servants.

"Thank you! Now tell me your news."

Anna spoke up first. "I decided to grow flowers to sell at the market with the money you gave me. Now I have ten times the original amount!"

"Well done, Anna! I trusted you with a small amount, and you were faithful. I'm putting you in charge of ten cities."

"Thank you, Master Judah!" said Anna.

"Reuben, tell me your story," invited Judah.

"Welcome home, Master Judah! I took the money you gave me and purchased a herd of milking goats. I've earned you five times more."

"Well done, Reuben! I gave you a small amount, and you were faithful. I'm putting you in charge of five cities."

"Thank you, Master," replied Reuben.

"Where is Thad? Is he here?" Judah asked.

"Right here, Master Judah," Thad said as he moved out of the shadows in the back of the courtyard.

"Tell me about your project. What did you do with the money I gave you?"

"It's right here," said Thad, producing a bundled piece of cloth from a bag that hung over his shoulder."

"I don't understand, Thad. These are the exact coins I gave you."

Reuben and Anna glanced at each other, worry on their faces.

"Master Judah, I knew you were a difficult man, so I was afraid. You take things you don't own and gather in a harvest from the work of others," Thad explained, then looked away.

"Thad, if you think I'm a difficult man," Judah began solemnly, "then the least you could have done is put the money in the bank so I could have collected the interest. I'm taking the money away from you and giving it to Anna."

Silence filled the courtyard as Thad left.

"I understand there are others who did not choose to give their loyalty to me," said Judah. "Some of the leaders that sit at the city gate did not want me to be their king. Please bring them to me. It's time that we talk."

Teaching Tips

1. Find the original story in Matthew 25:14–30 and Luke 19:11–27. How are the two versions of the story the same, and how are they different?

2. Who does Judah represent in this parable? Why do you think so?

3. Master Judah calls Anna and Reuben "faithful." Each one is rewarded. What does this teach about the kingdom of heaven?

4. Many people today openly talk about not believing in God or the return of Jesus. Help your children think about the reasons they would give people for the "hope that you have" in the promises of Jesus, as instructed in 1 Peter 3:15. Have your children write or draw their reasons in their journals.

5. Work with your children to plant some seeds in a pot or buy an already potted plant. Provide water and sunlight. Make a sign that says "God Gives Growth," and attach it to the pot. Put the plant in a place where you and others will see the living parable of God growing your faithful work and investment of time.

Summary

Jesus helps us to invest our time, talents, and treasure in working to share His love with others.

How to Get Another Job

Scripture

What is more, I consider everything a loss because of the surpassing worth of knowing Christ Jesus my Lord.

—Philippians 3:8

One day Jude, a property owner, called his manager to his office. "Obed, what is the truth of the rumor I've heard about you?"

Obed did not answer.

"I have heard that you are wasting my money. Unless you can assure me this isn't true, you are fired. Then I'll need you to bring me the accounting books."

Obed did not argue or plead his case as most servants would have done if they were fired. Instead, he wondered, *What can I do? I'm not strong enough to work on a farm and dig. I would be ashamed to beg. Jude is such a kind man. I know that he will not send me to jail or sell my wife and children as slaves. What can I do to take care of my family? Hmm. I know. I will do favors for Jude's debtors so one of them will give me a job.*

When he reached his office, Obed asked a servant to call some of the people who owed Jude money. "Please ask Josiah, Haman, and Seth to come and see me right away."

In a few minutes, Seth came into the office. "How much oil do you owe my master?" Obed asked.

This chapter is based on Luke 16:1–9 and Christ's Object Lessons, *chapter 26, " 'Friends by the Mammon of Unrighteousness.' "*

"Five hundred gallons," Seth answered.

"Here, write two hundred and fifty on the bill," Obed told him.

Seth wrote on the bill and signed it. Then he left.

Josiah came into the office.

"How many bushels of wheat do you owe my master?" Obed asked.

"Four hundred bushels," Josiah said.

"Here, write three hundred on the bill," Obed said.

Josiah wrote on the bill, signed it, and walked out.

Haman also arrived at the office.

"How many gallons of grape juice do you owe my master?" Obed asked.

"Six hundred gallons," Haman told him.

"Here, write four hundred on the bill," Obed said.

Haman wrote on the bill, signed it, and went home.

After adding the new receipts to the books, Obed carried them to Jude's office.

"Here are the books, Master," he said.

Jude looked at the books, carefully checking the pages. When he saw the receipts newly signed by Seth, Haman, and Josiah, he said to his former manager, "Obed, you have acted shrewdly. You have opened doors for yourself to get other jobs because these men are grateful to you. I cannot denounce what you have done without making myself look cruel and greedy. You have taken advantage of me, but you are very clever in your dishonesty."

Jude sat at his desk, thinking of the old saying, *Whoever is honest with little will be honest with much. And whoever is dishonest with little will be dishonest with much. I need to find a new manager—one as smart as Obed but also completely honest.*

Summary

God's approval of our choices is worth far more than praise from people.

Teaching Tips

1. Read this parable in Luke 16:1–9.

2. Compare this story with the parable of the prodigal son (Luke 15:11–32). Compare the characteristics of the master in this story with those of the father of the prodigal son.

3. Why does the manager cheat the master?

4. In this story, is Jesus praising the manager for cheating his master or for trusting in the goodness of the master? Why?

5. Talk with your children about the meaning of this story. Have your children write or draw in their journals what they have learned about God's character.

Attacked by Bandits

One day a lawyer asked Jesus a question. "What do I have to do to inherit eternal life?"

"What does the Law say?" Jesus replied.

"Love your God with all your heart and with all your soul and with all your strength and with all your mind, and love your neighbor as yourself," the lawyer stated.

"Good answer," Jesus said. "Do this and you will live."

The lawyer asked another question. "Who is my neighbor?" (see Luke 10:25–29).

Jesus answered his question with a story.

* * * * *

Jaden's head hurt. He touched the sore spot and looked at his hand. It was covered with blood.

"Where am I?" he wondered as he closed his eyes and went back to sleep.

Later, he heard someone walking near him, singing a hymn. He opened his eyes

This chapter is based on Luke 10:25–37 and Christ's Object Lessons, *chapter 27, " 'Who Is My Neighbour?' "*

Scripture

So in everything, do to others what you would have them do to you, for this sums up the Law and the Prophets.

—Matthew 7:12

THERE IS POWER IN KINDNESS!

and saw a priest. *Maybe the priest will see that I need help*, he thought. But the priest walked by on the other side of the road.

A few minutes later, Jaden heard another person walking along the road. He opened his eyes and saw a Levite. *Perhaps he will help me*, Jaden thought. But the Levite walked by on the other side of the road too.

Since the priest and the Levite didn't help me, will anyone help me? Jaden wondered, feeling more discouraged than before.

Jaden felt for his money belt, looking for the money he had brought with him to buy a new business in Jericho. It wasn't there. He felt around as best he could. The money was missing. *So I've been robbed as well as beaten. It's clear that no one will help me. I might as well try to get up*, he thought. However, getting up was too painful, and Jaden lay down, wondering what he could do as he fell asleep again.

The next time he woke up, he saw a Samaritan leaning over him. *A Samaritan? Maybe he's a robber too!* Jaden thought. He tried to yell, "Don't touch me," but no sound came out of his mouth.

Then the Samaritan brought him some water. "Try to drink," he encouraged.

Will this Samaritan try to poison me? Jaden thought. *I can't get much worse than I am now.* He sipped a little of the water and felt a tiny bit better.

The Samaritan washed the sore place on Jaden's head. He poured oil and wine over it and then wrapped it in a clean bandage. The stranger found other wounds and treated them also.

"Where were you going?" the Samaritan asked.

"To Jericho from Jerusalem," Jaden whispered. Then he thought, *This Samaritan treats me better than my own people.*

"Who attacked you?"

"I can't remember. My money is gone," Jaden whispered again.

"Don't worry. I'll take you to Jericho. You can ride on my donkey," the stranger said.

"No, you must not go to Jericho. Jews don't like Samaritans and might hurt you. They might think that you are the one who beat me and stole my money," Jaden whispered again.

"No, no; I'm not afraid. You need to go to Jericho, and you can't go alone," said the stranger. "I will help you. You will be safe."

"Yes, I will be safe. But maybe some angry person will hurt you," Jaden insisted.

However, the Samaritan continued to help—even supporting Jaden as he climbed on the donkey's back.

Jaden groaned with pain.

The kind Samaritan carefully chose level places on the road to make Jaden's ride easier. He led the donkey slowly, trying to make the journey less painful for Jaden. He had to put his arm around Jaden to keep him from falling off the donkey.

"I know of an inn in Jericho. The innkeeper knows me and will help us," said the stranger.

As they approached Jericho, young boys came out of the city, yelling at the Samaritan.

"Hey, you! Samaritan! Why are you helping this Jewish man? Are you the one who hurt him in the first place?"

Then an older man approached the Samaritan and Jaden, "Hello, stranger," he said. "Thank you for being kind to my countryman. Can I help you?"

The gang of boys, listening to the older man, stopped yelling and ran in the opposite direction.

"I am taking this man to stay at the inn on the street near the Jordan River. The owner has been kind to me before. I can trust him," the Samaritan explained.

"I know the place. I will hurry ahead to let him know that you are coming," the older man said as he walked away toward the river.

"Why are you being kind to me?" Jaden asked the Samaritan. "What is your name?"

"My name is Joaz. I would want someone to help me if I was hurt," he answered.

When Joaz and Jaden reached the inn by the river Jordan, the owner was waiting for them. "Joaz, a kind man said that you were coming with a man who was injured. I have fixed a room for the two of you," the innkeeper said.

"Are you also kind to Samaritans?" Jaden asked the innkeeper.

"Yes, I believe that God wants me to be kind to everyone," he said.

Joaz and the innkeeper carried Jaden to the room and laid him carefully on the bed. Then Joaz requested, "Please get Jaden some warm soup. Then he needs to rest and sleep."

In the morning, Joaz told the innkeeper, "Here is the money for our food and our room for last night. Jaden needs to stay here several more days before he will be ready to travel. When I come this way again, I will pay

Summary

Jesus helps His followers treat everyone with kindness.

you for his care. I know that you will take good care of Jaden."

"That will be fine. I know that you will pay me, Joaz. I trust you," said the innkeeper.

"Which road will be safer for me to take?" Joaz asked.

"We haven't had much trouble lately, but I think that you will be safer if you take the road by the river. Goodbye, Joaz. See you soon," the innkeeper advised.

"Thank you for helping us," Joaz said as he started down the road.

* * * * *

"Who was Jaden's neighbor?" Jesus asked the lawyer.

"The one who showed him mercy," the lawyer said.

"Go and do the same," Jesus told the lawyer.

Teaching Tips

1. Read this story in Luke 10:25–37.

2. Compare this story with the story of Philip and the Ethiopian (Acts 8:26–39).

3. What two characters could have helped the wounded man but didn't?

4. Why did Joaz the Samaritan choose to help the wounded Jewish man when people from their two cultures often didn't get along?

5. Work with your children to think of a family from another culture who needs to be welcomed and accepted. Then make a plan to befriend this family. If you don't know someone from another culture, consider helping children from another country learn about Jesus by donating money to missions. You might choose to sponsor a child in another country. You could exchange letters and cards with the child. If this project is too expensive for your family, consider sponsoring the child with two or three other families.

Pay for a Day

"I have never seen so many grapes in our vineyard as we have this year! The Lord has blessed us," said Jeshua to his vineyard manager, Zebulon.

"We need to harvest them tomorrow," insisted Zebulon. "If we wait a day longer, the grapes will begin to shrivel, and you didn't grow this crop for raisins. However, I'm worried."

"Why?"

"Well, usually, my assistant and I can manage the harvest by ourselves, but this year we'll need help."

"I have a solution! Early tomorrow morning I'll visit the marketplace to see whether there are men looking for work. I'll hire them to help you."

The next morning Jeshua woke up and dressed while it was still dark. He arrived at the market in time to watch the vendors setting up their stalls. Cucumbers, pomegranates, pistachios, and apples, along with a large variety of animals and woven blankets, all waited for the buyers who would arrive soon.

This chapter is based on Matthew 19:16–30; 20:1–16; Mark 10:17–31; Luke 18:18–30; and Christ's Object Lessons, *chapter 28, "The Reward of Grace."*

Beyond the stalls with goods for sale stood two men. It appeared they were waiting for work.

"Good morning!" Jeshua greeted. "Are you looking for work today?"

"We are indeed," said one of the men.

"That is good news," answered Jeshua. "If I paid you each a denarius, would you help my vineyard manager harvest grapes today?"

"That's a fair wage for a day of work. Yes, we'll help."

"Then follow me." Jeshua smiled, and together they walked back to his vineyard.

An hour later, Zebulon found Jeshua. "Excuse me, sir, but can I speak with you for a moment?"

"Sure, Zebulon. What do you need?"

"Well, we are working steadily to harvest the grapes. The two workers you hired this morning are helping, but we could use a few more. Would you see whether there are more men looking for work?"

"I'll head to the market right now. If I hurry, I can get there by nine. I'll be back as soon as I can."

Jeshua noticed that the market had many more buyers and sellers now. He struggled to see through the crowds. Finally, he saw four men standing close to where he had found the first two harvesters.

"Good morning!" Jeshua greeted. "Are you looking for work today?"

"We are indeed," said one of the men.

"That is good news," answered Jeshua. "If I paid you fairly, would you help my vineyard manager harvest grapes today?"

"Yes, we'll help," the men agreed.

"Then follow me." Jeshua smiled, and together they walked back to his vineyard.

Jeshua returned to the market at noon and again at three because Zebulon requested more help. He found five additional harvesters waiting for work. They agreed to work with Zebulon and followed Jeshua home.

Less than an hour after Jeshua had returned from his three o'clock visit to the market, Zebulon found him again. "Can I ask you for help just one more time?"

"Sure, Zebulon. What do you need?"

"The eleven workers you hired have worked hard today. The grapes have all been harvested. However, we are running out of daylight, and we need to get the grapes safely stored. If you could go back to the market and see if there might be two or three more workers that could help us finish up, I would be grateful."

"I'm on my way. If I hurry, I'll make it by five. I'll be back with more help as soon as I can."

Jeshua found most of the shoppers had left the market. The vendors were packing up, getting ready to leave. He looked around and saw three workers who looked a bit worried.

"Greetings!" Jeshua said. "Why are you still at the market?"

"No one has hired us," said one of the men.

"Well, then, come with me to my vineyard. We need help finishing up the harvest," answered Jeshua. "If I paid you fairly, would you help?"

"Kind sir, you are so generous. Our families will be able to eat tonight! Yes, we'll help!"

"Then follow me." Jeshua smiled, and together they walked back to his vineyard.

About an hour later, Zebulon found Jeshua. "Sir, I am happy to report that the harvest is complete. The extra workers you hired made a big difference."

"I'm so glad," Jeshua said. "Call them over so you can pay them. Give all of them a denarius for their work. Here is the money."

So Zebulon gathered the workers. He started by paying the harvesters who were hired last. "Here is a denarius for each of you."

"Thank you! Thank you so much!" each of them replied gratefully.

At last, he called the group who had been hired first. "Here is a denarius for each of you."

"Wait a minute!" said one. "We've been working hard all day long, and we only get a denarius? That's what you paid everyone—even the three who only worked the last hour of the day. This doesn't seem fair."

Jeshua overheard their comments and walked over to where they stood. "Friends, didn't you agree to work for a denarius?"

"Yes, but that's the same wage you gave to everyone. We should get more since we worked all day long—in the hot sun, no less."

"Are you upset with me because I am choosing to be generous?"

Jeshua and Zebulon walked them to the front gate of the property and watched them leave.

"You are generous, Master," Zebulon said to Jeshua.

"Always, Zebulon. Always."

Summary

Jesus generously gives us forgiveness and life forever in heaven with Him when we choose to follow Him.

Teaching Tips

1. This parable is found in Matthew 20:1–16. Compare these verses with Titus 3:4, 5. What do these verses help you understand about Jesus?

2. Who do the vineyard workers represent? What does their pay represent? Who is the vineyard owner?

3. Do the workers who started in the morning have a good reason to complain? Why, or why not?

4. Work with your children to figure out the pay for an eight-hour day for the jobs they would like to have when they grow up. How much difference in pay is there between working for one hour and working for eight hours? Ask how they would feel about their employers if they were paid for a whole day's work when they had only worked for one hour. Discuss how this idea connects with the story of the vineyard workers.

5. Work with your children to wrap a box as a present. Place the box where it can be seen every day. When a visitor to your house asks about the wrapped box, let your children explain that it is to remind everyone of God's gift of forgiveness.

The Bridesmaids

"Ima! Ima! Guess what!" Eva called to her mother as she hurried into the house.

"You know that Tirza and Obadiah are getting married soon. Tirza just asked me to be one of the girls who will escort her to the wedding. Isn't it exciting?"

Eva's mom, Zara, gave her a big hug. She said, "Come sit down with me. I want to tell you a story."

Mother and daughter settled down on the grass under the apple tree in the front yard.

"Ima, tell me the story, please," Eva insisted. "You know I love stories."

"I was just your age when my best friend, Hadassah, asked me to be one of the girls to escort her to her wedding. I was just as excited as you are today. There were ten of us. We prepared carefully so that everything would be ready for the wedding. Each girl had a lamp to carry in the procession back to the groom's house.

This chapter is based on Matthew 25:1–13 and Christ's Object Lessons, *chapter 29, " 'To Meet the Bridegroom.' "*

Scripture

Look, I am coming soon! My reward is with me, and I will give to each person according to what they have done.

—Revelation 22:12

"We waited and waited for Levi, the groom, and his friends to come that last evening. We knew that he had built a special room for Hadassah and himself to live in. The guests were already at his parents' home. We all became sleepy and napped. At last, we heard the shofar, the ram's horn trumpet, announcing the bridal party.

"Hurriedly, we rearranged our hair and our clothes. Then we trimmed the wicks on our lamps as they had burned out while we slept. I was alarmed because almost all the oil for my lamp was gone. We needed the lamps to see the path to the wedding and so that people could see our faces to recognize us," Ima continued.

"What did you do?" Eva asked.

"Five of us didn't have enough oil, so we asked the other girls whether they would lend us some of their oil. You can imagine how upset we were when they said no. They said that they didn't have enough oil to share with us and told us to go buy oil from one of the shops," Ima said.

"Did Levi arrive? Did Hadassah and the other girls leave without you?" Eva asked.

"We hurried off to a shop, banged on the door to awaken the shopkeeper, and waited while he grumbled and found us some oil. We heard the noise of the groom and his men's arrival at the bride's house. We saw the lights and all the excitement. We were very angry at ourselves for not bringing extra oil.

"At last, our lamps were burning brightly. As quickly as we could safely walk, we headed for Levi's house. When we finally arrived there, no one was outside, and the door was closed. I knocked on the door, hoping that we could still enjoy the party. The five of us called out, 'We're here now. Please let us in.' Levi answered us, 'I don't know you. It's too late. The party has already started.'

"Sadly, the five of us walked back to our homes. I don't know about the other girls, but tears were rolling down my cheeks because my disappointment was so great," Ima said as she finished her story.

Eva hugged her ima. "Thank you for telling me that story. You must have been very sad. I will be very careful to take extra oil for my lamp when I go to Tirza's wedding. I remember hearing Jesus say that He is the Groom and we, His followers, are the bride. What a beautiful way to describe the relationship between Him and us! Being ready for His return is far more important than being ready to go with the bride to a wedding."

Summary

We prepare for Jesus' return by listening to and learning from the Holy Spirit.

Teaching Tips

1. Find and read the original story in Matthew 25:1–13. Compare this story with the parable of the wedding banquet (Luke 14:15–24). How are these two stories the same, and how are they different?

2. How is Zara's story similar to the story Jesus told about the bridesmaids? How is it different?

3. What is the important lesson in Jesus' story about the bridesmaids?

4. Show your children pictures of family weddings. Explain how bridesmaids in your culture help a bride prepare for her wedding. Ask your children to write or draw in their journals about what they have learned.

5. Organize a group of children at church or school to act out this story while someone reads Matthew 25:1–13. Help the actors understand the meaning of the story so that they can portray it correctly to the audience.